DIGITALCOIN

HISTORY OF THE FIRST YEAR

A DECENTRALISED CRYPTOCURRENCY
PART OF THE "ALT-ERNATIVE" BOOK SERIES

CHRISTOPHER P. THOMPSON

Digitalcoin—History of the First Year

by Christopher P. Thompson

Book Author by Christopher P. Thompson

Book Design by C. Ellis

ISBN—13: 978-1534831490

ISBN—10: 1534831495

DIGITALCOIN

HISTORY OF THE FIRST YEAR

A DECENTRALISED CRYPTOCURRENCY
PART OF THE "ALT-ERNATIVE" BOOK SERIES

CHRISTOPHER P. THOMPSON

ABOUT THE AUTHOR

Christopher Paul Thompson is an avid cryptocurrency enthusiast from the United Kingdom. Born in Bradford, UK and academically educated at the University of York (BSc Mathematics). He has been a keen follower of past and current events in the crypto space since March 2013. His first book called Cryptocurrency "The Alt-ernative" A Beginner's Reference is the first book he has ever written.

Other titles currently available:

"Peercoin—History of the First Year"
"Reddcoin—History of the First Year"
"DigiByte—History of the First Year"
"Dogecoin—History of the First Year"
"GoldCoin—History of the First Year"

Other titles to be released soon:

"Quark—History of the First Year"
"Crypto Bullion—History of the First Year"
"Anoncoin—History of the First Year"
"WorldCoin—History of the First Year"
"Feathercoin—History of the First Year"
"Diamond—History of the First Year"
"Unobtanium—History of the First Year"

E-mail Contact: chris_thompson25@live.co.uk
Twitter Contact: https://twitter.com/MrSilverCider

CONTENTS

CONTENTS

INTRODUCTION

Cryptocurrency was born with the advent of Bitcoin. It was first mentioned in a research paper published online titled "Bitcoin: A Peer-to-Peer Electronic Cash System" with the real name or pseudonym Satoshi Nakamoto attributed to it. This paper was published on the 31st of October 2008. About two months later on the 3rd of January 2009, the Bitcoin network protocol was launched. This technological breakthrough was the beginning of a decentralized public ledger. It allows people to send value across the globe without the permission of a third party authority.

Since then, a growing number of people around the world have been introduced to or discovered cryptocurrency. Many cryptocurrencies have been launched over the following years since the introduction of Bitcoin. The name "alternative" was given to these cryptocurrencies after Bitcoin because they were developed, implemented and introduced to be used instead of or alongside Bitcoin. One could say, a choice of brand in cryptocurrency exists. People have discovered these either through word of mouth, by accident, through personal investigation or via the media. Nevertheless, it has changed the lives of many people. It has provoked the general public into asking innumerable questions about many issues based on subjects such as economics, politics, philosophy, mathematics and so on.

In this book, I hope to give the reader insight into how one particular alternative cryptocurrency began. Digitalcoin began in May 2013 as a Scrypt proof of work clone of Litecoin. This book, as well as other future books to be written on other cryptocurrencies, is a historical story of the first year. It covers the time from the initial announcement on Bitcointalk up until the blockchain had been publicly available for one year. In this case, from the 18th of May 2013 to the 20th of May 2014. It also describes the terminology one encounters in cryptocurrency such as proof of work mining, block reward, wallets and so on.

INTRODUCTION

I chose to write about just the first year for various reasons, some of which are:

- For almost all cryptocurrencies, the first year of their existence is the most defining period.

- If I had chosen to write a full history of Digitalcoin, I would be continuously playing catch up.

- Most other cryptocurrencies are not several years old yet, so I have limited the scope of all books on individual cryptocurrencies at this time.

- Currently I have a full-time job besides being a cryptocurrency author, so my time is unfortunately limited.

You may have bought this book because Digitalcoin is your favourite cryptocurrency. Alternatively, you may be keen to find out how it all began. I have presented the information henceforth without going into too much technical discussion about Digitalcoin. If you would like to investigate further, I recommend that you read material currently available online at the official website at www.digitalcoin.co.

If you choose to purchase a certain amount of Digitalcoin, please do not buy more than you can afford to lose.

Enjoy the book :D

WHAT IS DIGITALCOIN?

Digitalcoin is a cryptocurrency or digital decentralised currency used via the Internet. It is described as a payment network without the need for a central authority such as a bank or other central clearing house. It allows the end user to store or transfer value anywhere in the world with the use of a personal computer, laptop or smartphone. Cryptography has been implemented and coded into the network allowing the user to send currency through a decentralised (no centre point of failure), open source (anyone can review the code), peer-to-peer network. Cryptography also controls the creation of newly mined Digitalcoin units of account.

The Digitalcoin network protocol was created by using the source code inherent in the original Scrypt based coin called Litecoin. The developers of Digitalcoin altered the code to produce an alternative coin with a differing block reward schedule, block time, difficulty re-targeting algorithm and total number of expected coins. At the time of publication of this book, the hashing algorithm consists of three independent algorithms called SHA256, Scrypt and X11. This change occurred during the second year.

On the official website, the description of Digitalcoin is:

"Digitalcoin is a decentralized peer-to-peer cryptographic medium of exchange that is not controlled by any central authority. Digitalcoin is designed for security, stability, and ease of use. This regard for stability is inherent in the design of the economy and in the spirit of the community."

The slogan, besides others, used by the community to market the coin is:

"AN ANONYMOUS, INSTANT, AND SECURE DIGITAL CURRENCY"

WHY USE DIGITALCOIN?

Like all cryptocurrencies, people have chosen to adopt Digitalcoin as a medium of exchange through personal choice. An innovative feature of the coin, an affinity towards the brand or high confidence of the community could be reasons why they have done so. Key benefits of using Digitalcoin are:

- It is a useful medium of exchange via which value can be transferred internationally for a fraction of the cost of other conventional methods.

- Digitalcoin eliminates the need for a trusted third party such as a bank, clearing house or other centralised authority (e.g. PayPal). All transactions are solely from one person to another (peer-to-peer).

- Digitalcoin has the potential to engage people worldwide who are without a bank account (unbanked).

- Digitalcoin is immune from the effects of hyperinflation, unlike the current fiat monetary systems around the world.

On the official Digitalcoin website, the community describe "How One Can Use" the coin:

"Digitalcoin is optimized for performance and is one of the fastest ways to send and receive transactions in the world. Digitalcoin is a real, usable, and free to use currency with multiple vendors and ways to purchase a variety of items including hardware, software, Steam games, food, jewelry, precious metals, and more."

IS DIGITALCOIN MONEY?

Money is a form of acceptable, convenient and valued medium of payment for goods and services within an economy. It allows two parties to exchange goods or services without the need to barter. This eradicates the potential situation where one party of the two may not want what the other has to offer. The main properties of money are:

♦ **As a medium of exchange**—money can be used as a means to buy/sell goods/services without the need to barter.

♦ **A unit of account**—a common measure of value wherever one is in the world.

♦ **Portable**—easily transferred from one party to another. The medium used can be easily carried.

♦ **Durable**—all units of the currency can be lost, but not destroyed.

♦ **Divisible**—each unit can be subdivided into smaller fractions of that unit.

♦ **Fungible**— each unit of account is the same as every other unit within the medium (1 DGC = 1 DGC)

♦ **As a store of value**—it sustains its purchasing power (what it can buy) over long periods of time.

Digitalcoin easily satisfies the first six characteristics. Taking into account the last characteristic, the value of Digitalcoin, like all currencies, comes from people willing to accept it as a medium of exchange for payment of goods or services. As it gets adopted by more individuals or merchants, its intrinsic value will increase accordingly.

DIGITALCOIN SPECIFICATION

Since the birth of Digitalcoin, its coin specification has changed a few times. At the time of publication of this book, its current specification is:

Coin Symbol:	DGC
Unit of account:	DGC
Date of Announcement:	18th of May 2013 at 21:30:36 UTC
Genesis Block Generated:	6th of May 2013 at 19:09:44 UTC
Block Number One Generated:	20th of May 2013 at 09:57:27 UTC
Date of Launch:	20th of May 2013 at 09:57:27 UTC
Founder:	user "baritus"
Lead Developer:	Digitalcoin Foundation
Hashing Algorithms:	Scrypt, X11 and SHA-256
Timestamping Algorithm:	Proof of Work
Address Begins With:	D
Total Coins:	48,166,000
Block Time:	40 seconds
Difficulty Retarget Time:	40 seconds
Coins per Block:	5 DGC
Confirmations per Transaction:	Random
Pre-mine:	None

DIGITALCOIN MILESTONE TIMELINE

6th of May 2013	—Genesis bock timestamped at 19:09:44 UTC
18th of May 2013	—DGC Bitcointalk thread created at 21:30:36 UTC.
20th of May 2013	—First block explorer was created and launched.
20th of May 2013	—Official website www.digitalcoin.co went live.
20th of May 2013	—Block number one timestamped at 09:57:27 UTC.
23rd of May 2013	—Cryptsy was the first exchange to initiate DGC trades.
23rd of May 2013	—DGC Subreddit at .../r/digitalcoin founded.
26th of May 2013	—An updated wallet client released.
27th of May 2013	—Digitalcoin Paper Wallet Generator launched.
29th of May 2013	—Digitalcoin Online Marketplace launched.
10th of June 2013	—Crypto Trade was the second exchange to initiate DGC trades.
17th of June 2013	—Vircurex was the third exchange to initiate DGC trades.
22nd of June 2013	—Coins-e was the fourth exchange to initiate DGC. trades.
23rd of June 2013	—New forum www.digitalcoin.co/forums went live
28th of June 2013	—Market capitalisation surpassed $100,000 for the first time.
2nd of July 2013	—Official Digitalcoin Facebook Page was founded.
7th of July 2013	—Exclusive DGC exchange announced (in development)
31st of July 2013	—CoinEx was the fifth exchange to initiate DGC trades.
18th of August 2013	—CryptoAve (exclusive exchange) prototype unveiled.
25th of August 2013	—PhenixEx was the sixth exchange to initiate DGC trades.

DIGITALCOIN MILESTONE TIMELINE

4th of September 2013	—Digitalcoin support began at www.coinpayments.net.
7th of September 2013	—Version 0.2 of the wallet client released.
21st of September 2013	—Cryptsy introduced the DGC/LTC trading pair.
13th of October 2013	—Version 1 wallet client released (mandatory).
13th of October 2013	—Official Twitter Account created at .../DigitalcoinDGC.
15th of October 2013	—Android Wallet App (alpha) released on the Google Play Store thanks to user "ahmed_bodi".
30th of October 2013	—Portable USB Project added to www.indiegog.com.
2nd of November 2013	—Fixed Android Wallet App (alpha) released on the Google Play Store.
5th of November 2013	—Reward per block reduced from 20 DGC to 15 DGC.
18th of November 2013	—The lowest Bitcoin Satoshi value of one unit of DGC account recorded at 300 for the entire first year.
23rd of November 2013	—Portable USB Campaign on Thunderclap ended.
26th of November 2013	—Market capitalisation surpassed $1,000,000.
2nd of December 2013	—CryptoAve status update posted on Facebook.
6th of December 2013	—Number of .../r/digitalcoin subscribers surpassed 100.
7th of December 2013	—Closed beta testing of CryptoAve began.
13th of December 2013	—Online marketplace Coinmart announced.
14th of December 2013	—DGC began active trading on the BTC38 exchange.
14th of December 2013	—DGC began active trading on the Bter exchange.
14th of December 2013	—All time high market capitalisation attained.
19th of December 2013	—Version 1.1 of the wallet client released (mandatory).
26th of December 2013	—Phase one of beta testing (trading engine) complete.
30th of December 2013	—Block number 625,800 surpassed.

DIGITALCOIN MILESTONE TIMELINE

2014

7th of January 2014	—DGC added to the block explorer at http://blockr.io.
12th of January 2014	—Open beta testing of CryptoAve began.
18th of January 2014	—Another paper wallet designed by user coinnoisseur".
20th of January 2014	—First Tweet by user "baritus" (@OfficialBaritus).
20th of January 2014	—First DGC Dice Game created by user "Hazard".
26th of January 2014	—First lightweight wallet announced by user "ShimalH".
27th of January 2014	—User "baritus" interviewed by "Follow The Coin".
1st of February 2014	—Revised launch (10th Feb) of CryptoAve announced.
1st of February 2014	—Version 0.1 of the lightweight Dub client released.
4th of February 2014	—CryptoAve open beta testing announced as complete.
8th of February 2014	—Official DGC Forum back online after spam attack.
9th of February 2014	—Version 0.1.1 of the lightweight Dub client released.
10th of February 2014	—Tentative launch (14th Feb) of CryptoAve announced.
10th of February 2014	—DGC began trading on the exchange Bitchanger.
10th of February 2014	—DGC began trading on the exchange Cryptorush.
15th of February 2014	—Transaction malleability issues fixed for CryptoAve.
17th of February 2014	—Official launch (21st Feb) of CryptoAve announced.
18th of February 2014	—DGC began trading on the exchange PmToCoins.
18th of February 2014	—DGC began trading on the exchange OpenEx.
21st of February 2014	—Exclusive exchange CryptoAve went live.
24th of February 2014	—Attendance at the Scholastic Auditorium confirmed.
24th of February 2014	—DGC began trading on the exchange CryptoAltex.
27th of February 2014	—New design of the Digitalcoin logo unveiled.
28th of February 2014	—DGC added to the MintPal voting list.

DIGITALCOIN MILESTONE TIMELINE

1st of March 2014	—The launch of Coinmart postponed indefinitely.
2nd of March 2014	—Initial formation of the Digitalcoin Foundation.
4th of March 2014	—A dedicated Digitalcoin TipBot went live on Reddit.
6th of March 2014	—USD verification (not trades) went live on CryptoAve.
7th of March 2014	—Number of .../r/digitalcoin subscribers surpassed 500.
9th of March 2014	—560k DGC announced as stolen from user "baritus".
17th of March 2014	—DGC began active trading against BTC on Prelude.
21st of March 2014	—USD deposits permitted at Prelude.
23rd of March 2014	—Revamped design of the official website launched.
23rd of March 2014	—Version 2.0 (Core) of the wallet client announced.
25th of March 2014	—DGC began active trading against USD on Prelude.
25th of March 2014	—Updated Android Wallet App released.
9th of April 2014	—The source of attacks on CryptoAve identified.
9th of April 2014	—DGC added to the website http://bravenewcoin.com.
9th of April 2014	—Andrew Davidson spoke at the Scholastic Auditorium.
10th of April 2014	—Vault of Satoshi announced future trading of DGC.
13th of April 2014	—DGC added to the website http://coingecko.com/en.
22nd of April 2014	—Andrew Davidson's speech uploaded to YouTube.
26th of April 2014	—The dgc.sryptmining.com mining pool closed down.
27th of April 2014	—DGC began active trading on the Swaphole exchange.
2nd of May 2014	—DGC Foundation Survey created at Surveymonkey.
7th of May 2014	—A peak in the number of Reddit subscribers at 572.
8th of May 2014	—CryptoAve back online after approx. one month.
18th of May 2014	—One year since the announcement of Digitalcoin on Bitcointalk.
20th of May 2014	—Last block (1st year) timestamped at 09:56:17 UTC.

19

DIGITALCOIN BLOCKCHAIN

Every cryptocurrency has a corresponding blockchain within its decentralised network protocol. Digitalcoin is no different in this sense. A blockchain is simply described as a general public ledger of all transactions and blocks ever executed since the very first block. In addition, it continuously updates in real time each time a new block is successfully mined. Blocks enter the blockchain in such a manner that each block contains the hash of the previous one. It is therefore utterly resistant to modification along the chain since each block is related to the prior one. Consequently, the problem of doubling-spending is solved.

As a means for the general public to view the blockchain, web developers have created block explorers. The first block explorer for Digitalcoin was made available at the domain http://dgc.p2pool.nl/chain/Digitalcoins. It was announced as being accessible on the 20th of May 2013. However, it no longer exists.

Since the inception of the first block explorer, other websites have been created. Currently available block explorers include the following:

- https://chainz.cryptoid.info/dgc/;

- http://dgc.blockr.io/;

- https://prohashing.com/explorer/Digitalcoin/;

To be specific, the first two block explorers are officially recognised and trusted. One can easily access these sites by visiting http://www.digitalcoin.org and then clicking on the "Network Information" hyperlink in the top right hand corner.

DIGITALCOIN BLOCKCHAIN

Block explorers tend to present different layouts, statistics and charts. Some are more extensive in terms of the information given. Some statistics include:

- **Height of block**   —the block number of the network.

- **Time of block**   —the time at which the block was timestamped to the blockchain.

- **Transactions**   —the number of transactions in that particular block.

- **Total Sent**   —the total amount of cryptocurrency sent in that particular block.

- **Block Reward**   —how many coins were generated in the block (added to the overall coin circulation).

Below is a screenshot of block number one from the block explorer at https://chainz.cryptoid.info/dgc/:

Details for Block #1

Hash	45b2559dbe5e5772498e4170f3f1561448179fa90dd349e68e891766878dea2e
Date/Time	2013-05-20 09:57:27
Transactions	1
Value Out	2.0 DGC
Difficulty	0.00024414
Outstanding	2.0 DGC
Created	2.0 DGC

Transactions   Raw Block

Hash	Value Out	From (amount)	To (amount)	
70ab0da9321a...	2.0 DGC	Generation + Fees	DSzQNKVjiSABZyKgq4cnfrvm6Jnfe4QGKK	2.0 DGC

PROOF OF WORK (PoW) MINING

Proof of work mining is a competitive computerised process which helps to maintain and secure the blockchain in such a way as to verify transactions and prevent double spending.

In the general sense of cryptocurrency, those who participate in the activity of mining are called miners. They are general members of the cryptocurrency community who dedicate processing power (hash) of their computers towards solving highly complex mathematical problems and verifying transactions. This process upholds the integrity and security of the network. As such, miners are described as protectors of the network. Each transaction (held within a certain block) is validated before adding it to the blockchain. By doing this, they are rewarded (as an incentive) with newly generated mined coins or transaction fees. These coins are issued by the software in a transparent and predictable way outside of the control of its founders and developers. A miner can be based anywhere in the world as long as they have an internet connection, sufficient knowledge of how one mines and the hardware/software required to do so.

Miners use GPUs (Graphical Processing Units) or CPUs (Central Processing Units) to process transactions by hashing. Also, Application Specific Integrated Circuits (ASICs) allow miners to use customised hardware for faster and lower power mining.

Since its launch on the 20th of May, Digitalcoin has always had proof of work as timestamping. On the 9th of December 2014, the hashing algorithm switched from solely Scrypt to three independent algorithms (Scrypt, SHA256 and X11).

At the time of publication of this book, miners compete to successfully find blocks which generate five DGC each.

BLOCK TIME OF DIGITALCOIN

The block time is the average time taken for the network to successfully generate a certain block either by proof of work or proof of stake. Both the reward and time of all blocks generated dictate how the circulation of coins grows over time.

Originally, the block time of the network protocol was pre-determined to permit miners to find one block every twenty seconds (on average). This remained the case until the mandatory hard fork at block number 523,800 kicked in. The first twelve blocks timestamped to the blockchain on the 20th of May 2013 were:

Block Number 1	09:57:27 UTC		Block Number 7	09:57:34 UTC
Block Number 2	09:57:30 UTC		Block Number 8	09:57:34 UTC
Block Number 3	09:57:31 UTC		Block Number 9	09:57:35 UTC
Block Number 4	09:57:32 UTC		Block Number 10	09:57:36 UTC
Block Number 5	09:57:32 UTC		Block Number 11	09:57:37 UTC
Block Number 6	09:57:34 UTC		Block Number 12	09:57:37 UTC

As is evident above, it took ten seconds to find the first twelve blocks. This was the result of low initial difficulty and very high processing power committed by miners to the network protocol at the beginning.

BLOCK REWARD DISTRIBUTION TABLE

As time progresses, a certain number of coins (reward) are generated each time a block has been mined, verified and added to the blockchain. As is almost often the case, the reward per block decreases to a lower value at a pre-determined block number. As is evident in the table below, the initial block rewards available to miners were initially set low as a means to deter early hoarding and sell offs.

On the 7th of September, a mandatory wallet client (version 0.2) was released in order to combat the wild swings in difficulty (how hard it is to mine DGC). This change came into effect at block number 476,280 on the 10th of October 2013.

On the 13th of October, a mandatory wallet client (version 1) was released. Effective from block number 523,800 on the 5th of November, it changed the coin specification (see page 72).

During the first year, a total of 15,364,543 DGC were mined in the space of 856,902 blocks. Here is the current block distribution table of Digitalcoin:

Initial Block	Last Block	Number of Blocks	Reward	Total	Cumulative Total
1	1,079	1,079	2	2,158	2,158
1,080	2,159	1,080	1	1,080	3,238
2,160	3,239	1,080	2	2,160	5,398
3,240	4,319	1,080	5	5,400	10,798
4,320	5,399	1,080	8	8,640	19,438
5,400	6,479	1,080	11	11,880	31,318
6,480	7,559	1,080	14	15,120	46,438
7,560	8,639	1,080	17	18,360	64,798
8,640	476,279	467,640	20	9,352,800	9,417,598
476,280	523,799	47,520	20	950,400	10,367,998
523,800	625,799	102,000	15	1,530,000	11,897,998
625,800	1,027,999	402,200	15	6,033,000	17,930,998
1,028,000			5		

DIGITALCOIN WALLETS

A wallet is basically a piece of software that can be used on a personal computer, tablet or smartphone. It allows users to store Digitalcoin as well as execute transfers of DGC with other users. Alternatively, it can be described as a means to access the coins from the inseparable blockchain (public transaction ledger). The wallet cryptographically generates and holds the public and private keys necessary to make these transactions possible. The software can be accessed, downloaded and installed from the official website by clicking selecting the "Choose Wallet" option from the "Wallet" dropdown menu at:

- http://www.digitalcoin.org/index.php

Digitalcoin wallets have been developed to work on the operating systems Windows, Mac OS X and Linux. Currently, there are several types of wallet available to the community. These are:

- A wallet client which can be installed on one's own personal computer:

| Microsoft Windows | Apple Macintosh | Linux Distributions | Android OS |

Alternatively, it is possible to store one's coins in an online secure wallet. Two such wallets, officially recognised by the community, are at https://www.coinwallet.co and http://coinpayments.net (see image on page 62). Unfortunately, the former site has closed. Sensible advice given to people is not to hold large amounts of DGC in online wallets. However, it is a convenient way to gain access to the DGC held.

Another method by which to store DGC is by creating an offline wallet. Usually in the form of paper, it shows the public key and a covered up private key.

FIRST YEAR DIGITALCOIN EXCHANGES

Throughout the first year, sixteen known cryptocurrency exchanges added Digitalcoin to their trading platform. As is evident below, the vast majority of exchanges have closed down due to dubious activities, successful hacking attacks carried out upon them or other reasons. Only Vircurex, BTC38 and Bter still offer active trading of Digitalcoin as of the 21st of June 2016.

The following table lists the dates on which active trading of the coin began:

Cryptsy	BTC and LTC	CLOSED	23rd of May 2013
Crypto Trade	BTC	CLOSED	10th of June 2013
Vircurex	BTC	ACTIVE	17th of June 2013
Coins-e	BTC	CLOSED	22nd of June 2013
CoinEx	BTC and LTC	CLOSED	31st of July 2013
PhenixEx	BTC	CLOSED	25th of August 2013
BTC38	BTC and CNY	ACTIVE	14th of December 2013
Bter	BTC and CNY	ACTIVE	14th of December 2013
Bitchanger		CLOSED	10th of February 2014
Cryptorush	BTC	CLOSED	10th of February 2014
PmToCoins		CLOSED	18th of February 2014
OpenEx		CLOSED	18th of February 2014
CryptoAve	BTC, LTC and USD	CLOSED	21st of February 2014
CryptoAltex		CLOSED	24th of February 2014
Prelude	BTC and USD	CLOSED	17th of March 2014
Swaphole	BTC	CLOSED	27th of April 2014

CURRENT DIGITALCOIN EXCHANGES

A cryptocurrency exchange is a site on which registered users can buy or sell DigiByte against BTC, LTC, USD and so on. Some exchanges require users to fully register by submitting certain documentation including proof of identity and address. On the other hand, most exchanges only require users to register with a simple username and password with the use of a currently held e-mail account.

On the 21st of June 2016, there were nine known exchanges or methods to buy/ sell/trade Digitalcoin. At this time, BTC38 was the exchange on which the highest daily trade volume was occurring. Bittrex was the second most popular platform.

Current cryptocurrency exchanges which actively allow users to trade DGC are:

Exchange	Location	Traded Against
BTC38	China	BTC and CNY
Bittrex	United States	BTC
Bleutrade		BTC
Safecex		BTC
Cryptopia	New Zealand	BTC and LTC
Alcurex	Finland	BTC
Vircurex		BTC
Bter	China	BTC and CNY
CoinExchange		BTC

DIGITALCOIN COMMUNITY

A community is a social unit or network that shares common values and goals. It derives from the Old French word "comuntee". This, in turn, originates from "communitas" in Latin (communis; things held in common). Digitalcoin has a community consisting of an innumerable number of individuals who have the coin's well being and future goal at heart. These individuals almost always prefer fictitious names with optional corresponding "avatars". Notable members of the community are users "baritus", "Tsquared", "disclaimer201" and others.

At the time of publication, there are social media sites on which discussion and development of Digitalcoin take place. These are:

- **Facebook**   -https://www.facebook.com/DigitalCoinDGC
- **Official Forum**   -https://forum.digitalcoin.co
- **Reddit**   -https://www.reddit.com/r/digitalcoin
- **Twitter**   -https://twitter.com/DigitalcoinDGC
- **Bitcointalk**   -https://bitcointalk.org/index.php?topic=1127380.0

In essence, the community surrounding and participating in the development of Digitalcoin is the backbone of the coin. Without a following, the prospects of future adoption and utilisation are starkly limited. Digitalcoin belongs to all those who use it, not just to the developers who aid its progress.

FIRST YEAR HISTORY OF DIGITALCOIN

LIST OF CHAPTERS

LAUNCH OF THE DIGITALCOIN BLOCKCHAIN

MAY 2013

I.   Bitcointalk forum thread created for Digitalcoin.

II.   First known block explorer at http://dgc.p2pool.nl/chain/Digitalcoins.

III.   First exchange called Cryptsy began to offer trades in Digitalcoin.

IV.   A new version of the Digitalcoin wallet client was made available.

V.   Digitalcoin online marketplace was launched.

On the 18th of May 2013 at 21:30:36 UTC, a Bitcointalk forum thread was created by a user known by the fictitious forum name "baritus". This thread was originally titled "[ANN]digitalcoin, A Currency for a Digital Age.". About eight minutes later, the first response to this thread was posted by user "runam0k" who was quoted as saying:

"Tell me more!"

User "baritus" responded to the short post above by saying more details are coming as development wraps up. He also said he was working on a release paper which would detail the objectives of the Digitalcoin Project.

Digitalcoin was born as a fork of (derived from) the Litecoin source code.

Block #0 (Reward 0 DGC) May 6th 2013 at 07:09:44 PM UTC

As can be seen above, the genesis block (the first block timestamped to the blockchain, but not block number one) was generated twelve days previously. However, the cryptocurrency community were not able to mine DGC until the 20th of May 2013. The developers estimated the launch at 7:00 AM GMT on this day.

A question was asked by user "syn999" who said:

"does this offer something new from other ones?"

On the 18th of May at 22:38:27 UTC, user "baritus" replied by saying:

"Yeap, almost instant transactions, quick difficulty adjustment, steady rewards, no pre-mining, fair launch, simple and transparent."

On the following day, testing of the code resumed to make sure everything would function as required. Screenshots of the software (Windows executable) were posted besides commentary to keep people informed of progress made. User "baritus" enquired if people could volunteer as testers in order to make sure the launch would go as smoothly as possible.

On the 19th of May at 14:55:14 UTC, user "baritus" said:

"Please contact me if you are interested in making a pool, block explorer, or any software integrating digitalcoin. There will be a bounty.

Thank you."

In order to help people get ready for the public launch of the coin, user "baritus" was willing to post a "How To Guide" for mining.

One day prior to the public launch (the time from which coins can be mined) of the blockchain, the community were made aware of the initial block rewards. Unlike other cryptocurrencies, the block reward was set low to begin with. It would then increase until it reached twenty DGC per block. This was viewed by the developers as being fairer for miners as it reduced early hoarding and large initial sell offs. In addition to the aforementioned, the average block time was set as twenty seconds.

A table of the initial block reward distribution was as follows:

Initial Block	Final Block	Reward (DGC)	Total Cum DGC
1	1,079	2	2,158
1,080	2,159	1	3,238
2,160	3,239	2	5,398
3,240	4,319	5	10,798
4,320	5,399	8	19,438
5,400	6,479	11	31,318
6,480	7,559	14	46,438
7,560	8,639	17	64,798
8,640		20	

On the 20th of May at 09:55:53 UTC, user "baritus" said:

"Launched. Website: digitalcoin.co"

Shortly after this website (the first official Digitalcoin website, but now re-directs to www.digitalcoin.org) had been announced as being live, block number one was mined:

Block #1 (Reward 2 DGC) May 20th 2013 at 09:57:27 AM UTC

> **Block #8,639 (Reward 17 DGC) May 20th 2013 at 06:35:01 PM UTC**

> **Block #8,640 (Reward 20 DGC) May 20th 2013 at 06:35:10 PM UTC**

From block number 8,640, the reward per block would remain at 20 DGC for the next three years. However, this would change at a later date.

On the 20th of May at 20:35:52 UTC, user "fran2k" announced that he had created an exchange/escrow service. There was enthusiasm within the community to start trading DGC with Bitcoin (BTC), Litecoin (LTC) and so on. He posted the following:

> "GDocs Exchange here! Also Escrow Service.
>
> https://bitcointalk.org/index.php?topic=211243
>
> Only DGC/LTC
>
> I'm looking forward to add BTC as well, is there a way I can feed the BTC/LTC ratio into the spreadsheet??
>
> Tips are Welcome"

On the 21st of May at 01:37:28 UTC, user "baritus" said:

> "Appended the following to difficulty section of the original post to better explain difficulty adjustment.
>
> Every 1080 blocks (6 hours @ 20 seconds per block), the network scales the difficulty accordingly. Example: If target is 6 hours and it took 3 hours to find 1080 blocks, difficulty will increase 200%."

On the 22nd of May at 02:40:31 UTC, user "baritus" said:

> "There's no rush for an exchange.
> We will need one soon though to keep up with the transactions."

The developers of the coin wanted to make sure the technical aspects of the code were functioning properly before efforts were made to push for exchange adoption. However, there were people who wanted a means by which to buy and sell the coin without resorting to untrustworthy trading on forums with unidentified individuals, or using the recently created GDocs Exchange created by user "fran2k".

Also on the 22nd of May at 03:14:31 UTC, user "baritus" said:

> "Coming today:
>
> 1. digitalcoin dedicated forum: A new forum dedicated to digitalcoin will be established. Moderator applications are open.
> 2. digitalcoin foundation: The foundation will be set up with the goal to further the integration of digitalcoin into society.
> 3. digitalcoin developer newsletter: A newsletter connecting the developers of digitalcoin will open for registration."

User "techbytes" responded to the above announcement by saying:

> "Nice! I will donate 100 DGC for every 1000 I mine to the foundation."

On the 23rd of May, DGC began to actively trade on its first cryptocurrency exchange called Cryptsy. It launched three days previously and was based in Delray Beach, Florida, USA. Trading ceased on the exchange on the 14th of January 2016.

> https://www.cryptsy.com/markets/view/26

On the 23rd of May at 19:30:48 UTC, user "baritus" said:

> "Update
>
> I have finished work on the QT source and it is now available for all to compile. Please try it out and let me know how it goes.
>
> The repository has been updated."

Shortly after the above update, user "baritus" asked for a few testers of a future official Digitalcoin forum. Community members, including user "redplegm", were quick to pledge their support. Also, user "techbytes" asked about the status of the anticipated Digitalcoin Foundation and bounty programs. User "baritus" answered by saying:

> "The bounty programs needs more donations, which makes it hard to setup bounties. There's less than 900 DGC donated so far to the development.
>
> Currently, I am working on the forum and some client optimizations.
>
> The foundation and developer newsletter will be delayed due to the current situation requiring all my attention."

On the same day, two Digitalcoin related websites went live:

> https://www.reddit.com/r/digitalcoin
> http://digitalcoin.org/

On the 24th of May, user "baritus" was pleased that everything was progressing nicely. Working alongside a couple of other developers, he decided the time was right to begin creating applications integrating Digitalcoin. He created an online poll on Bitcointalk according to which a "Marketplace" won 29 out of 48 votes. Other options were an online wallet, mobile applications and games.

On the following day, the developers announced the initial development of the Digitalcoin Marketplace. A fully capable trading platform, the separation of virtual and tangible goods, and special tools for media sales would be included. The only method of accepted payment would be Digitalcoin.

Further announcements on this day were:

- The development of an online wallet to make it easy for people to get started with Digitalcoin.

- A 3,200 DGC development bounty was established thanks to donations from the community. The first person to provide either an interesting game using DGC as currency, a paper wallet, a DGC classifieds site or a payment processing platform would receive it (latter would receive 1 BTC extra). Taking into consideration the bounties were funded by donations, they would grow as more donations were sent.

On the 26th of May at 17:48:01 UTC, user "baritus" said:

> "UPDATE
>
> A new version of the digitalcoin client is available for download.
>
> If you use Windows, a new binary is available from the first post. Users who compiled from source will find the git repository updated.
>
> This commit updates the checkpoints."

It is unknown whether a version number was assigned to this update. Nevertheless, user "baritus" asked members of the community to test this new update. He had tested it rigorously and had added checkpoints to make sure the client would remain on the correct blockchain of the Digitalcoin network protocol.

On the 27th of May, user "baritus" encouraged users to move some activity to the official Digitalcoin forum (original one before the current one). A forum on which a lively discussion and innumerable giveaways would occur was highly sought after.

On the 27th of May at 14:26:12 UTC, user "maxpower" said:

> "I just uploaded a Mac version of the Digitalcoin wallet. The download link is in my Mac Wallets thread: https://bitcointalk.org/index.php?topic=216672
>
> Enjoy, and let me know how it works!"

Users still had to compile the Linux client themselves on the 27th of May.

On the 28th of May at 13:10:06 UTC, user "baritus" said:

> "Starting work on the advertising platform today.
>
> QueenB will be joining me for more development on DGC related software, so you should see good fast results." 😊

On the 29th of May, user "baritus" was pleased to announce the completion of the online marketplace launched at http://dgcmarket.com. He also made the community aware of the ongoing progress of the advertising platform. It was scheduled to be released on the 7th of June 2013. It would allow someone to buy advertising and pay people, who view the advertisements, using Digitalcoin. Furthermore, advertisers would have geographic targeting options and would be guaranteed unique, interested viewers. He thanked the Digitalcoin Community for making all this possible.

On the 30th of May at 01:09:34 UTC, user "baritus" said:

> "I do know that the coin does not have enough current users for a massive marketplace. But I want to provide it for anyone who wants it.
>
> Also, I already have a plan to get thousands of fresh DGC users and buyers. It's already in the works."

Auctions were listed on the DGC Marketplace pretty much immediately. There was an instance of illegal substances being auctioned/sold, but this was removed (they didn't want a bad reputation like Silk Road). Categories added to the marketplace on the last day of May were "Jewellery" and "Video Games".

Other events which occurred in the month of May were:

- On the 20th of May, the first known block explorer for DGC was released at http://dgc.p2pool.nl/chain/Digitalcoins. It does not exist anymore.

- A donation wallet address for development and integration was published on the 20th of May (DHgXvhswV9j3t9VTKu1QfAu6kYM1HHD5sJ).

- On the 22nd of May, Digitalcoin was added to www.bitgrenade.net.

- On the 24th of May, user "zacho56" created the first Digitalcoin Wiki at http://www.DGCwiki.com.

- User "QueenB" received the first development bounty of 3,200 DGC on the 27th of May. He had created the first Digitalcoin Paper Wallet Generator at http://digitalcoin.co/paperwallet.html (see image below).

- Supporters of DGC were able to vote for the coin's addition to the exchange Vircurex during May. The poll at https://bitcointalk.org/index.php?topic=215284.0 closed on the 31st of May.

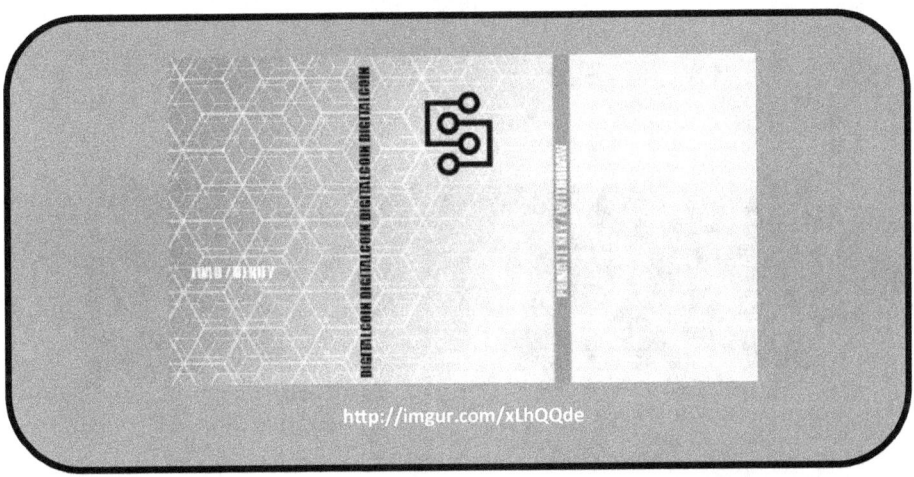

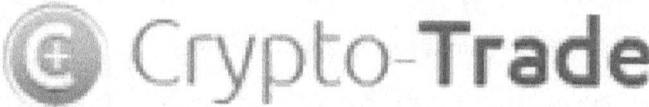

Vircurex

NEW OFFICIAL DIGITALCOIN FORUM WENT LIVE

JUNE 2013

I.   An exchange called Crypto Trade began to offer Digitalcoin trading.

II.   Digitalcoin added to the site www.coinmarketcap.com.

III. An exchange called Vircurex began to offer Digitalcoin trading.

IV.   A new official Digitalcoin forum went live.

V.   Market capitalisation surpassed $100,000.

Some users on the official Digitalcoin Bitcointalk forum thread pledged, or promised wholeheartedly, to donate their first auction revenues to the DGC Dev Fund. On the first day, the Bitcoin Satoshi value of one unit of DGC account on Cryptsy was 18,302.5 according to the website www.cryptocoincharts.info. A low of 16,604 and a high of 20,001 were also recorded on that day.

On the 2nd of June at 18:26:01 UTC, user "baritus" said:

"Please donate to the digitalcoin development foundation. The newest initiative is creating a gamer's auction site and promoting it for virtual item sales. The advertising platform is also on track for Friday completion.

DGC Dev Fund: DHgXvhswV9j3t9VTKu1QfAu6kYM1HHD5sJ"

On the 3rd of June at 21:11:42 UTC, user "baritus" said:

"I also made a program to simulate DGC creation.

You can see the results here:
https://bitcointalk.org/index.php?topic=209508.msg2333025#msg2333025"

On the 4th of June at 10:41:48 UTC, user "r32godzilla" said:

"Yep dgc is performing quite nicely. Steady climb in value on Cryptsy rather than a regular pump and dump like some other alts. Looking forward to Baritus bringing online the dgc advertising platform and his other excellent ideas for dgc. Dgc is really starting to gather some good momentum now."

According to www.cryptocoincharts.info, BTC Satoshi values of DGC (Cryptsy) were:

Date	Price	Low	Open	Close	High	Volume (DGC)
1st June	18,203.5	16,604	16,604	20,001	25,000	140,067.9581
2nd June	22,500.5	18,710	20,001	25,000	35,490	103,813.0806
3rd June	25,855	21,000	23,700	28,010	38,895	113,312.1312

On the 5th of June at 02:15:09 UTC, user "baritus" said:

"DGC will have a new developer joining the team! He will be an additional core developer and help maintain, upgrade, and continue digitalcoin's progress. Welcome Hazard 😊 !"

On the 5th of June at 19:43:38 UTC, user "baritus" said:

> "NEWS:
>
> The advertising platform will be completed tomorrow, ahead of schedule by one day.
> Website access will be phased until stability is confirmed.
> If you would like to be one of the first testers, please message me."

Four days later, the website www.coinmarketcap.com incorporated Digitalcoin. Besides many other cryptocurrencies, the market capitalisation, the fiat value per one unit of DGC account, the total number of DGC in existence could, from now on, be checked regularly. One can also view historical market capitalisation charts of DGC as well as those of hundreds of other cryptocurrencies.

Also on the 9th of June at 19:15:29 UTC, user "baritus" said:

> "Important Announcement:
>
> Cryptsy.Com exchange has had a double deposit bug/issue that resulted in people doubling up their balances. All trading is shut while they look into the issue.
>
> It seems that many took advantage of the opportunity to dump DGC they don't own on the market. I hope Vern can restore the market back to normal."

Between two and three hours later, trading of DGC on Cryptsy was back to normal and the value of the coin recovered quickly from the exchange code errors. Cryptsy had suffered some kind of glitch during which time trading deposits malfunctioned.

On the 10th of June at 13:42:00 UTC, user "neotrix" said:

> "DGC has been added on crypto-trade.com for trading against BTC.
>
> https://crypto-trade.com"

Crypto Trade was the second exchange to offer its users active trading of Digitalcoin. After numerous delays, it launched on the 26th of May 2013 with BTC, LTC, NMC, PPC, TRC, FTC, CNC and DVC as the initial tradable coins.

On the 12th of June, Digitalcoin was added to its third exchange called Vircurex. However, they hadn't activated live trading of the coin at this time.

On the 16th of June, user "baritus" said a new forum (including some very interesting features) will be up today. This did not materialise.

On the 17th of June at 12:50:44 UTC, user "baritus" announced the following:

"Now trading on vircurex.com!"

On the same day at 13:12:30 UTC, in response to the active trading of Digitalcoin on Vircurex, user "Xmansk" said:

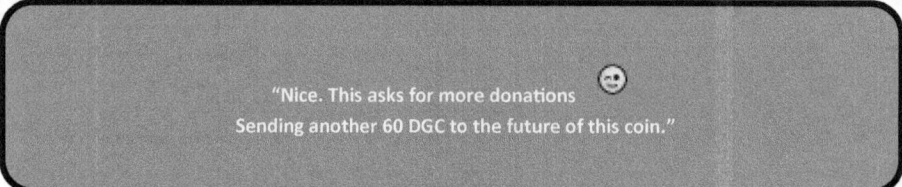

"Nice. This asks for more donations 😄
Sending another 60 DGC to the future of this coin."

On the 22nd of June at 18:02:57 UTC, user "baritus" said:

"Added coins-e to the exchange list."

On the 23rd of June at 14:53:57 UTC, user "baritus" said:

> "New forum is up at http://digitalcoin.co/forums, come visit and win free DGC!"

The first post on this new official forum was submitted by user "pr9me" who said:

> "Hey guys! Looks like I'm first here. DGC...one small step for crypto, one giant leap for crypto-kind! Have a good one! Pr9me 8)"

Another person who had also registered was called user "r32godzilla". He encouraged others to do the same.

Further discussion at the end of the month was about getting Digitalcoin added to the exchange called BTC-e. It was an immensely popular exchange at the time, and other cryptocurrencies were vying to get on there too. Only a handful of coins have been successfully added to BTC-e. On the 27th of April 2016, Ethereum and Dash trading pairs DSH/BTC, ETH/BTC, ETH/USD and ETH/LTC were initiated there.

Other events which occurred in the month of June were:

- On the 1st of June, Satoshi Dice for DigitalCoin was released at http://www.dgcdice.com by user "ethought".

- On the 5th of June, user "dreamwatcher" notified the community that DGC had been included on CryptoCoin Explorer at www.cryptocoinexplorer.com or, more specifically, at http://dgc.cryptocoinexplorer.com.

- On the 6th of June, the advertisement platform went live in public beta at http://digiclick.co/.

- Block number 100,000 timestamped on the 11th of June at 01:16:08 UTC.

- On the 28th of June, the market capitalisation surpassed $100,000.

"A Currency for a Digital Age"

DISCUSSION OCCURRED ABOUT CHANGING
THE BLOCK REWARD DISTRIBUTION SCHEDULE
JULY 2013

I.   Facebook group founded at www.facebook.com/DigitalCoinDGC.

II.   Digitalcoin logo graphics published.

III.   Value of Digitalcoin surged from the 7th of July to the 11th of July.

IV.   Discussion about changing the block reward distribution schedule occurred.

V.   An exchange called CoinEx began to offer Digitalcoin trading.

On the last day of June, user "baritus" thanked all those who had donated towards the ongoing Digitalcoin Development Fund.

On the 1st of July at 00:38:55 UTC, user "r32godzilla" said:

> "Yep its nice to see people helping out where they can and supporting dgc because obviously they have faith in whats happening with it and the developments you and
>
> the team are making for it."

Also at the beginning of the month, user "baritus" needed people to help translate the website into Chinese, Hindi, French, German, Spanish, Italian and Japanese. If anyone could translate it into any other language, he was happy to hear from them too. People were able to enquire about a bounty on the official Digitalcoin forum.

On the 2nd of July, the official Digitalcoin Facebook group was created at https://www.facebook.com/DigitalCoinDGC. It is still the current group, but activity there has become very slim. The graphic on page 46 was the first cover image for the group (uploaded and posted on the 2nd of July 2013).

On the 7th of July, user "baritus" had been working, alongside the community, on a DGC/BTC/LTC/SRC/ARG exchange with fiat capabilities . He felt the time was right to announce the completion of the trading engine (testing still required). He made it clear that the exchange was required for future services/ideas in progress. For example, DGC/SRC/ARG investor option issuing services. (the exchange was not operational or accessible at this moment in time).

On the same day, the Bitcoin Satoshi value of one unit of DGC account began to rise substantially. Below is a table showing the values and corresponding daily trading volumes (in DGC) on three popular exchanges:

	Cryptsy	Cryptsy	Crypto Trade	Crypto Trade	Vircurex	Vircurex
	Price	Volume	Price	Volume	Price	Volume
7th July	27,980.5	123,210	28,000	1,288.67	27,899.5	8,684.28
8th July	29,380.5	158,456	27,750	19,071.4	27,785.5	2,351.79
9th July	33,400.5	341,235	31,750	8,989.17	31,736	9,096.20
10th July	46,310.5	713,220	47,000	40,094.6	49,990	27,635.9
11th July	54,045	459,302	72,999	42,347.8	53,989.5	26,797.2
12th July	55,683	322,019	55,500	3,406.37	51,128	3,841.13

source: www.cryptocoincharts.info

As an approximation, the market capitalisation of Digitalcoin increased from $81,000 to $240,000 from the 7th to the 11th. It went on to reach ~$280,000 three days later. This was an all time high until the 21st of November 2013.

On the 9th of July at 13:06:03 UTC, user "BitcoinFX" said:

"I've mentioned in this thread and via PM to Baritus that I'm in the process of producing some promotional items and products for digitalcoin (and some other alt. coins in fact)...

Forum member tjb0607 has very kindly produced some quality high-resolution vector graphics for Digitalcoin and is happy for the community to reuse them as required.

Download Link:
http://www.mediafire.com/download/irt4rapykvgpth8/Digitalcoin-Logos.zip

I have sent 20 XPM to tjb0607 and propose to send an additional 100 DGC myself (as an extra thank you) if anyone else would consider donating or perhaps matching my offer in increments, as a bonus for producing these excellent graphics.

tjb0607 DGC Address: DBqPXWoop6wCwjrCDqRNWok6vynHbofEqy

My DGC Address: DRaZkmtgLHxnSFBvQAr1pMNji2hhaqyWaG

Cheers"

Alongside their corresponding text logos, three coin logo designs were published:

In light of the graphics produced, user "jbmiller10" said:

> "Sent tjb0607 100 DGC and sent you a few as well! Thanks for the work y'all!"

As promised, user "BitcoinFX" sent 100 DGC to user "tjb0607" too.

On the 10th of July at 10:55:55 UTC, user "techbytes" said:

> "Sent 100 DGC to each address. Thank you both for your support and looking forward to your digitalcoin products.
>
> -tb-"

User "baritus" described the graphics as nice. He wanted bumper stickers created.

On the 11th of July at 14:27:50 UTC, user "r32godzilla" said:

> "Looks cool I should get one to take to work!"

User "BitcoinFX" went onto say:

> "That's great! I'll keep you posted for when the stock arrives with myself, then I'll have an exact purchase price including shipping.
>
> I'm also looking at printed USB wristbands, flipcards (credit card size USB's) and some rounded stick designs, but I'll see how these go first and make a separate poll for voting on designs.
>
> If anyone else is interested then please drop me a PM. Cheers."

Despite the official Facebook group being active for over one week, user "r32godzilla" said the following on the 15th of July at 14:38:44 UTC:

"New Digital Coin facebook page up. Please add your 'Like' if your on FB!

https://www.facebook.com/DigitalCoinDGC

Cheers" ☺

On the 15th of July at 21:16:27 UTC, user "disclaimer201" said:

"I really hope the community is stronger than a possible attacker. But is it? Litecoin hashrate is 28 Gh/s right now. DGC hardly 1, while DGC has the largest market cap of any POW scrypt coin behind litecoin (safe), and feathercoin (already successfully attacked).

Even a small fish ltc pool owner could attack DGC for breakfast right now, for totally unreasonable, or reasonable motivations such as protecting ltc from serious competition in the future. Bitcoin is safe (sha256), Litecoin is safe (too high hash rate), Feathercoin is toast, all other coins are either sha256 or Proof of Stake (Novacoin, PPC...) I know this sounds like FUD, but I'd be really happy if there were measures of protecting against a 51% attack.

DGC would likely be the next target, and I don't see how any ltc pool operator would suffer from that (if he does ltc a favor with it), or even be found out to be behind such an attack.

1	Bitcoin	$ 1,129,886,759	$ 98.95	11,418,775	BTC	+3.55 %
2	Litecoin	$ 58,364,578	$ 3.00	19,466,654	LTC	+5.42 %
3	Namecoin	$ 3,338,505	$ 0.56	6,014,143	NMC	+4.43 %
4	PPCoin	$ 2,973,268	$ 0.15	19,639,354	PPC	-6.23 %
5	Novacoin	$ 1,282,148	$ 4.14	309,767	NVC	+3.17 %
6	Feathercoin	$ 881,039	$ 0.087	10,118,050	FTC	+5.87 %
7	Terracoin	$ 565,937	$ 0.18	3,195,210	TRC	+12.03 %
8	Devcoin	$ 333,066	$ 6.8e-05	4,878,270,050	DVC	-3.29 %
9	Freicoin	$ 266,730	$ 0.012	22,644,509	FRC	+5.43 %
10	Digitalcoin	$ 205,112	$ 0.042	4,848,386	DGC	-25.74 %"

On the 25th of July at 19:43:29 UTC, user "theBee2112" said:

> "I've been supporting and mining this coin since its release. 80,000+ coins/day is just going to make them less valuable, as nobody seems to want to buy them.
>
> It's all miners who want to dump, and nobody else seriously wanting to buy. I wouldn't want to buy them either, especially after all the hype from btc-e, and nothing exciting happening in the past while. If it doesn't make it to another exchange, or devs don't make something new for it, it'll end up just like CNC.
>
> What ever happened to that DGC bank idea?"

On the same day at 20:04:31 UTC, user "baritus" said:

> "I'm working on it.
>
> The rate might be too high and require an adjustment down."

Again, on the 25th of July at 20:26:48 UTC, user "mr_random" said:

> "History will not look back kindly at digitalcoin if the dev arbitrarily decides to reduce the block reward to increase scarcity and please investors."

On the following day, a fundraiser was announced by user "techbytes" via a Bitcointalk thread titled "[ANN][DGC] Fund Raiser to take DGC to the next level | Goal is 25K DGC". On the 27th of July at 04:30:37 UTC, user "techbytes" said:

> "We reached our goal in less than 26 hours. DGC community rocks!! Thank you all for your contributions and for believing in DGC. -tb-"

On the 27th of July at 13:23:14 UTC, user "baritus" said:

> "Hello,
>
> I would like to know how the community feels about decreasing the DGC mining rewards. Additionally, it would be helpful to know by how much you think they should be decreased.
>
> Thank you."

Following on from previous opinions about decreasing the reward per block, user "disclaimer201" continued the conversation. He thought changing the rules would be disrespectful to those future individuals who wanted to support the coin. It would profit early adopters by making their coins more valuable. He went onto say it would be similar to some kind of "pre-mine". In conclusion, he did not take kindly to forcing success on the coin via reduced block rewards (a coin will either succeed or fail via other methods). He also said it was important to ensure the community is in full agreement of any changes, but not just the current community, the future one as well.

On the 28th of July at 12:59:27 UTC, user "baritus" responded to user "disclaimer201" about the current issues:

> "I'm just gauging community opinion with the poll, you can be assured no decisions are ever made in this community without input from all members. I definitely see both sides of the argument and I am currently siding with keeping it as is or a slight decrease (10-20%).
>
> Nevertheless, polls are one of the few ways of gathering information so don't be surprised to see them coming up. It doesn't mean anything but an opinion gauge.
>
> Good discussion, if anyone has anything else to add, please do."

An argument occurred between user "baritus" and "mercSuey" too. User "mercSuey" accused him of being a price manipulator of the coin and utterly clueless. User "baritus" said user "mercSuey" was "fermenting ignorance".

On the 31st of July at 16:11:27 UTC, user "BitcoinFX" announced the following:

"Ref. my forum post:
https://bitcointalk.org/index.php?topic=209508.msg2706284#msg2706284

The 50x 2GB (1.87 GB Usable Approx.) USB Slender Flashdrives printed with the digitalcoin logo have arrived with myself today!

I'm looking to sell around 10 of the 50 units for just digitalcoin, with the rest being placed as ebay auctions and on other online market places.

If you are interested in purchasing one with digitalcoin then please PM me with quantity and your country of residence for accurate p&p pricing etc. First come first served.

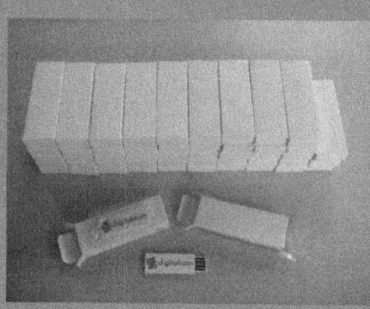

Very happy with the high print quality and compact size!

N.B. These are 2GB USB Flashdrive storage / wallet backup devices.
They are _not_ USB mining devices."

User "jbmiller10" was very enthusiastic about the produced USB flash drives. He described them as being really sleek. User "BitcoinFX" replied by saying:

> "Thanks.
>
> I've had 3 people interested from the US thus far.
>
> Maybe someone can organize a group buy ? It would save on the shipping costs to the US from the UK and will help reduce the price point per. unit."

On the 31st of July at 19:10:34 UTC, user "erundook" said:

> "DGC is now listed at https://coinex.pw exchange "

This was the fifth cryptocurrency exchange to add Digitalcoin. In addition to the exchange, a corresponding mining pool was a sister website of CoinEx. On the 17th of March 2014, CoinEx was hacked and, soon after this event had occurred, they ceased operations. Fortunately, some users were able to withdraw their deposits.

Other events which occurred in the month of July were:

- On the official Digitalcoin forum, user "Digiminer" notified the community that the coin had been getting requests for addition to BTC-e.

- On the 24th of July, the official Facebook group at https://www.facebook.com/DigitalCoinDGC now had 30 likes. There was an original Facebook group at https://www.facebook.com/DigitalCoin, but this has no recorded content or posts on it.

CRYPTOAVE EXCHANGE PROTOTYPE UNVEILED

AUGUST 2013

I.   A symbol for Digitalcoin mentioned.

II.   A total of 163,895.9 DGC donated to the DGC Dev Fund in eleven days.

III.   Was the difficulty re-targeting period too long?

IV.   CryptoAve unveiled as the exclusive upcoming proposed exchange.

V.   An exchange called PhenixEx began to offer Digitalcoin trading.

At the beginning of August, discussion resumed about the DGC USB flash drives. User "smscotten" enquired how much it would cost (DGC) to bulk send a few to the USA. He was willing to buy some so as to sell them on to interested US buyers. However, he thought user "techbytes" would be a more responsible community member. Later on, user "BitcoinFX" confirmed that user "techbytes" had ordered and paid for more than ten Digitalcoin USB flash drives.

Also on the first day of August, user "splicer" on the official Digitalcoin forum asked if a symbol for the coin (such as $ or £) had been discussed.

On the 3rd of August at 11:53 UTC, user "baritus" replied to "splicer by saying:

> "I'm not sure if a symbol is needed since the logo is the representation. DGC is also available as a shortening."

On the 3rd of August at 14:55:02 UTC, user "BitcoinFX" said:

> "Re: Topic: [ANN][DGC] Fundraiser to take DGC to the next level | 100K DGC Donated -
> https://bitcointalk.org/index.php?topic=262648.0
>
> I'll donate 10% DGC on any sales of my 2GB digitalcoin USB Flashdrives if purchased with
> DGC before Midnight GMT tommorow - 4th August 2013.
>
> See: https://bitcointalk.org/index.php?topic=209508.msg2840188#msg2840188"

On the 26th of July at 02:10:00 UTC, user "techbytes" created a separate Bitcointalk thread titled "[ANN][DGC] Fund Raiser to take DGC to the next level | Goal is 25K DGC". User "baritus" said the funds will be used 70/30 for the bank/exchange. The target was surpassed in less than twenty six hours. On the 3rd of August, over 100,000 DGC had been donated. At that moment, the top five donors were:

> User "techbytes" 20,325.275419
> User "TheCryptoPanda" 15,000
> User "Lloydimiller4" 13,250
> User "everybodyclapyohands" 10,000
> User "Ianfeusst" 10,000

On the 6th of August at 00:28:47 UTC, user "techbytes" was quoted as saying:

> "The bonus shares are now closed. Just 11 days, DGC community poured in over 163,000
> DGC. With such strong community support, I see a bright future for DGC.
> Thank you everyone for your support. We are all in it for the long run. As a token of
> appreciation, everyone on the list who donated 5000 DGC or more will receive one 2GB USB
> Flashdrives printed with the digitalcoin logo. For everyone else, you can order one when I
> have them in my hands. More details later." -tb-

On the 17th of August, there were worries that the difficulty re-targeting time/ period was too long to counteract the wild swings in hash occurring at mining multipools. User "baritus" said the network was handling things well for the time being. On the 18th of August at 22:01:52, user "Cryptos2go" said:

"I wouldn't worry about it too much, the devs will either make changes or they won't.

DGC works well enough imo, it will be fine as it is."

On the 18th of August at 22:27 UTC, user "baritus" posted the following on the official Digitalcoin forum. He said:

"Hello,

We are ready to unveil the first prototype of CryptoAve.Com. The exchange is still under heavy construction and the website will remain restricted except to developers. I will update as the design evolves and more pages are finalized. As you can see from the dummy text, this is ongoing.

Features:
-Trade BTC/LTC/DGC/ARG/SRC for each other and for USD
-Merchants can accept any currency through the built in payment processor
-Advanced instantaneous trading
-Fast deposits and withdrawals of fiat

I would appreciate feature requests, comments, and anything else you have to say.

Thank you and I hope we can change the crypto landscape together."

Also on the 18th of August, user "Aggrophobia" asked if the "bank" was nearly ready. In response, user "baritus" at 23:45:35 UTC said:

"The bank will be integrated in the exchange.
Checkout the exchange here: https://bitcointalk.org/index.php?topic=277241.0"

To coincide with the announcement of CryptoAve, an article was written by user "DannyDisco" titled "CryptoAve Prototype Unveiled! New Crypto Exchange With Fiat Options". The full article was:

"The long awaited screen shots of the new exchange from the Digitalcoin developers have been released. The new exchange will dawn the name "CryptoAve" and will give users the possibilities of trading from fiat to BTC/LTC/DGC/ARG/SRC and vice versa. It will also include a payment processor to allow merchants to easily integrate these coins as a payment option on their websites. This is definitely a step in the right direction for cryptocurrency lovers everywhere. The teaser screenshot looks slick, professional and incredibly promising. We are eagerly waiting for more and will keep you posted throughout it's development."

Here are some of the features you can expect:

- Trade BTC/LTC/DGC/ARG/SRC for each other and for USD

- Merchants can accept any currency through the built in payment processor

- Advanced instantaneous trading

- Fast deposits and withdrawals of fiat

- Shares of the exchange will be sold for DGC on the exchange itself

Followed, by the teaser screenshot:

On the 22nd of August at 14:44:15 UTC, user "baritus" said:

> "2 block retarget is idiotic. A better algorithm which takes into account more variables is the solution. I'm testing various options including capping the maximum difficulty drop. However, every solution comes with new problems.
>
> I also expect DGC to outgrow these issues with the marketing campaign now fully funded. The exchange will be designed in such a way as to provide a gateway for new adopters. It's easier to promote a method of making money than it is to promote a form of currency."

On the 24th of August, user "DannyDisco" on the official Digitalcoin forum was concerned that people were not able to post feedback or replies to threads created in the "Announcement Section". He pointed out the following:

> "I suggest you either open up the possibility to reply to threads in the announcement section... Or... post a separate thread for each announcement in the general forums and link to it in the announcement.
>
> I think that would really stimulate and engage the community and give these forums a real kick start."

Less than two hours later, user "baritus" concurred and lifted the restrictions.

On the 25th of August, DGC was added to the exchange called PhenixEx.

On the following day, user "baritus" posted two updates:

1.   You can buy CryptoAve exchange shares for DGC at digitalcoin.co/forums.

2.   An update of DGC will likely be released within the next three weeks to address the issue of profitability hopping pools."

At the end of the month, ongoing development plans for the coin were an exchange, payment processor, bank and poker website. Once these had been completed, other services such as a more advanced marketplace were planned. User "baritus" was very enthusiastic of the future prospects of the coin. Lots of promise and optimism was evident from members of the community too.

VERSION 0.2 OF THE WALLET CLIENT RELEASED
SEPTEMBER 2013

I.   Digitalcoin support began on payment processor at www.coinpayments.net.

II.   Version 0.2 of the wallet client released.

III.   Another new article written by user "DannyDisco".

IV.   First comment posted by user "kenel" on the official DGC Bitcointalk thread.

V.   Cryptsy initiated/introduced the trading pair DGC/LTC.

On Cryptsy, the value of Digitalcoin had decreased from about 27,556 BTC Sat on the 25th of August to about 16,100 BTC Sat on the first day of September. The vast majority of daily trading volume was occurring on this exchange.

On the 1st of September 08:42:11 UTC, user "r32godzilla" said:

> "The sooner dgc gets this update to combat multipools the better. Add to that everyone dumping for BTC while its high and its pain right across the board on alt coins.
>
> Looking forward to the exchange and things to settle down again soon hopefully."

Also on this day, user "baritus" stressed that Digitalcoin and Securecoin were the only coins he had been working on. He did not develop Argentum, but did maintain it when its developer could not. A DGC wallet client update was scheduled soon.

On the 4th of September at 00:11:14 UTC, user "baritus" said:

> ### UPDATES:
>
> 1. DGC is now supported on https://www.coinpayments.net/. I've also updated the pool list, let me know if I missed yours.
>
> 2. DGC is the primary currency of the upcoming CryptoAve exchange and the only currency supported for exchanging CryptoAve shares.
>
> 3. New investors are joining DGC and you should see the buy orders building up.
>
> 4. DGC will be updated so difficulty rises a maximum of 100% and drops a maximum of 50%. More details to be announced within the next couple of days.

Six hours after the above update, user "Xmansk" gave his/her opinion. He thought that solving the difficulty re-targeting issues should take the highest priority.

On the 7th of September at 19:18:19 UTC, on a separate Bitcointalk thread, user "baritus" announced a mandatory update to the wallet client. Version 0.2 (Windows + [Mac (thanks to user "maxpower")] had been released:

> "Hello,
> This is a mandatory update for all digitalcoin users.
>
> Profitability Hopping
> Recently, pool hopping software has made it easy for people to negatively affect crypto-currencies without a second thought. This update attempts to address that issue by capping the maximum difficulty rise at 100% and the maximum drop at 50%. This should help to stabilize the difficulty and lower if not eliminate the negative effects of such websites and software.
>
> ...FAQs...
>
> Other Additionally, the update makes client improvements and builds on the stability and security of the client.
>
> You must update before block 476,280. That is the difficulty protocol switching point."

Besides the aforementioned wallet client release, an article was published by user "DannyDisco" titled "Digitalcoin Releases Mandatory Client Update To Combat Against Profit Hopping Pools". The full article was:

"Digitalcoin has released a mandatory update (v 0.2) to help combat against the raising concerns of the effects of profit hopping pools. Pools such as Multipools and Middlecoin have taken the crypto mining world by storm. Full of profit seekers seeking to get the best possible bang for their mining buck are flocking to these pools which automatically switch to mine the most profitable coin. This becomes an issue because a sudden surge of hash power gets dumped on a coin all at once and greatly affects the coin's difficulty rating. Most of the time, leaving loyal miners earning less and less and missing out on low difficulty spikes

Digitalcoin will address these issues by capping the maximum difficulty rise at 100% and the maximum drop at 50%. This should help to stabilize the difficulty and lower if not eliminate the negative effects of such websites and software. This should eliminate radical difficulty fluctuations and reduces the highs and lows and eventually eliminate the advantage these profit seeking pools have on the coin. The update also makes client improvements and improves on the stability and security of the client.

Good on Digitalcoin for always being innovative and active in resolving whatever issues may arise. Clients must be updated before block 476,280. (Current block 418,331). We can't wait to see this client in action. You can download the new client from the following locations:

Windows: http://digitalcoin.co/download/digitalcoin-qt-V0-2.zip

Linux: http://digitalcoin.co/download/digitalcoinSource-V0-2.zip"

On the 10th of September at 14:28 UTC, user "RunningmanZ" had noticed that the Digitalcoin Marketplace (launched on the 29th of May 2013) had become very inactive. As a means to attract interest, he proposed incorporating a seller/buyer of the week award. These people would then be rewarded with a specific number of DGC. User "baritus" responded later that evening:

> "The market will get a full revamp once the current projects are completed."

On the 15th of September at 04:25:48 UTC, user "kenel" posted his first comment on the official Digitalcoin Bitcointalk thread. He said:

> "I'd like to know the economics (macro, micro, behavioral) behind people's assumptions that none of the changes will work.
>
> Didn't realize we were all trained economics professionals....."

His comment was in reference to the ongoing discussion about the change in the code attaining to the new difficulty specification in the network protocol. Some people were sceptical of the change achieving the required results.

On the 17th of September at 21:22:19 UTC, user "baritus" said:

> "The blocks until update were decided to give everyone enough time to update. Everyone needs advanced notice for a hard fork."

On the 21st of September, Cryptsy initiated the trading pair DGC/LTC on their exchange platform. From now on, alongside direct trading with Bitcoin, users were able to buy Digitalcoin directly with Litecoin.

On the 23rd of September at 14:11:03 UTC, user "baritus" said:

> "Please make sure to update if you haven't already.
>
> Also, there are a lot of interesting things happening at http://digitalcoin.co/forums"

There were only three posts on the official Digitalcoin Bitcointalk thread from the 23rd of September to the 30th of September. Discussion had shifted towards the official forum.

On the 30th of September at 22:53:19 UTC, user "Pmalek" said:

> "DGC again taking some serious beating today record low. All because of that 200k sell wall @ 0.0001398 . Someone is loading up before november maybe?"

According to www.cryptocoincharts.info, the Bitcoin Satoshi values of one unit of DGC account on four separate exchanges, on the 30th of September, were the following:

	Price	Low	Open	Close	High	Volume (BTC)
Cryptsy	12,252	10,000	13.004	11,500	13.190	38.7042
Vircurex	14,791	11,820	14,599	14,983	17,961	1.68882
Coins-e	14,000	14,000	14,000	14,000	14,000	0.00947198
Crypto Trade	13,000	13,000	13,000	13,000	13,000	0.00054093

VERSION 1 OF THE WALLET CLIENT RELEASED

OCTOBER 2013

I.   Difficulty update to wallet client began at block number 476,280.

II.   Announcement of hard fork (version 1) at block number 523,800.

III. Twitter Page https://twitter.com/DigitalcoinDGC went live.

IV.   Article titled "Digitalcoin, the Diamond in the Rough" published.

V.   Alpha version of the Digitalcoin Android Wallet App released.

It had become more apparent that there had been a recent increase in "profit hopping pools" and "profit seekers". People, who did not hold the long term interest of the coin, were selling their Digitalcoin for Bitcoin straightaway. As a result, user "baritus" said the following:

"The current inflation rate is not sustainable, regardless of difficulty changes. At 80,000 coins a day, that's 360 BTC added monthly at a rate of only 0.00015 DGC/BTC. It would be about 720 BTC to sustain 0.00030 DGC/BTC. Well, it would be added if it was mined by holders, but the mining landscape is now all about profit taking. A large portion of that money is being sucked out of the DGC economy. For that reason, an inflation rate of 25% the market cap is not going to work, regardless of whatever the difficulty."

On the 2nd of October, fixes were well underway to improve the coin specification.

Sustainability was the most important consideration for the dev team. As the value of DGC decreased, miners were less inclined to direct hashing power towards the network. Both the value and the generation rate determine mining profitability.

On the 7th of October at 05:54:41 UTC, user "r32godzilla" said:

> "Nice work Baritus on the latest upcoming V1 update for DGC. Can't wait to see these in action."

On the following day, user "baritus" created a Bitcointalk thread titled "[ANN] DGC V1 Overhaul and Network Adjustments + GIVEAWAY". After lengthy discussion, the community decided a reduction in the block reward was needed. User "baritus" had spent the last few days testing different candidates. A decision was made to reduce the block reward from 20 to 15 DGC as well as increase the block time from 20 to 40 seconds. He also said that "version one" would not be released for at least one week after V0.2 takes effect. This turned out to be not the case.

Two days later, the difficulty code adjustments in version 0.2 took precedence:

> **Block #476,280 (Reward 20 DGC) October 10th 2013 at 07:36:08 AM UTC**

On the 10th of October at 12:56:54 UTC, user "baritus" said:

> "The update was a success and the network didn't have any issues adjusting to the specs.
>
> The DGC V1 update should be similarly straightforward since I'll be using the same hard-forking method for the most part."

On the 10th of October at 22:59:07 UTC, user "baritus" said:

> "The website is now translated into French and Russian. If you are willing to translate, I will add any language that is contributed.
>
> I am offering a 300 DGC bounty per language translation as well."

A relevant news article on http://cryptosource.org was written and then published by "CryptoMaster" titled "Digitalcoin Difficulty Fix Update Successful". The full article was:

> "Early this morning, the Digitalcoin difficulty fix update took place without a hitch. In fact, it went better than expected. One of the largest profit switching pools had forgotten to update their client with over 800 MH/s pointing at the wrong blockchain were unsuccessful in forking the chain. This goes to show how successful the Digitalcoin developers were in updating their client. Usually, such a high hashrate would be able to take over a coin and cause it to fork. Instead, this large pool was left mining an invalid chain and finding no blocks for just over 8 hours.
>
> The fix issued is a deliberate attempt to try and ward off said profit seeking pools. The fix will limit the difficulty increase to a maximum of 100% and a maximum decrease of 50%. This is to limit the wild difficulty swings that would occur when one of the profit pools would dump all its hashing power on the coin temporarily. The swings would fly up to 5, then back to near 0 when they were done.
>
> So far so good! Here's to Digitalcoin! Good Job!"

On the 13th of October at 14:14:52 UTC, user "baritus" said:

> "Make sure to update your clients to V1. Download links are in the first post."

Prior to the above post submitted on the official Digitalcoin Bitcointalk forum thread, user "baritus" had created a separate thread on that same forum titled "[DGC] DigitalCoin V1 Release | Mandatory Update". This post can be seen on the next page of this book.

On the same day, the official Digitalcoin Twitter Page was created at https://twitter.com/DigitalcoinDGC. Besides other social media platforms, having an official presence on Twitter was welcomed by many people. Also on this day, a few of the coin's future plans were reiterated.

On the 13th of October at 12:52:51 UTC, user "baritus" announced:

"Hello,

This is a multi-faceted hard fork and as such it's important that all DGC users update as soon as possible.

Update Details
Rewards: 15 coins per block
Block Time: 40 seconds
Blocks to Retarget: 108 block retarget time (~72 min)
Other: UPNP support enabled, a new checkpoint is added, and the alert system has been updated.

You must update before block 523,800 or the digitalcoin network will no longer accept your client.

Thank you, Baritus"

An article was published by "Hazard" on the 14th of October titled "Digitalcoin, the Diamond in the Rough". The full transcript was as follows:

"I'll take a break from the usual altcoin bashing and do something a little less abrasive today – talk about a coin with favorable prospects. Digitalcoin (DGC) was one of those coins that was launched during the altcoin flood back in May. While coins of this era were typically defined by egregious premining/instamining and generally poor launches, DGC was about the only one that had a fair launch with no premine. DGC was pre-announced days in advance (a rarity, in it's time), and it's launchtime graphs are damn near picture perfect:

...(SEE APPENDIX)...

A steadily increasing supply along with a steadily increasing hashrate – these are the things indicative of a fair launch. It's been about 5 months since then, and DGC is still chugging along nicely. The community behind it is among the largest, as evidenced by it's 200 page long main thread. Many services already exist, among them, payment processing and web wallets.

The developer, Baritus, has remained surprisingly active as well, pushing out incremental updates and working on various projects to further the coin. The most ambitious of these being the Free Bank of Digitalcoin and CryptoAve, an exchange platform. Shares of CryptoAve will be traded exclusively in DGC, which will undoubtedly boost demand for the coin.

About 2.6 million DGC are produced each month (20 coins @ 20 second blocks), and at the current price of 0.00014, this puts ~360 BTC worth of downward pressure on the market. Yet, the price has remained surprisingly stable for a while now, so this indicates that a lot of money is flowing into DGC. It's important to note that in the upcoming v1.0 update block reward is being slightly reduced and block time is being increased to 40 seconds, effectively halving coin generation. Assuming cash inflow remains the same, the price of DGC should trend upward as a result.

My one real gripe with this coin is that not a whole lot is changed from the litecoin base. Block time and the coin distribution timeline are among the biggest of changes. I've talked with Baritus about this, and his design philosophy is such that he doesn't want to reinvent the wheel, just make a better version of it. So far, I think he's done a good job at accomplishing that. His involvement with the community and the scope of the projects he's working on give me little reason to doubt his competence.

Overall, the pros outweigh the cons, and DGC is a good coin. Unlike some other coins out there, no gimmicks are used to lure people in. It's just a good solid base, with a strong backing behind it. With v1.0 coming soon, and CryptoAve nearing completion, this coin is less of a risky investment than most. It's one of the few altcoins that meets all my requirements for a good coin: A fair launch, a solid developer, and a good community.

Have a coin that you'd like me to take a look at next? Let me know."

In response to the article written by user "Hazard", user "r32godzilla" said:

> "Nice article mate.
>
> Solid writeup with some good information. As mentioned by someone else you might want to add the adjusted block reward from 20 to 15.
> I really believe dgc is primed to join the big league in the not too distant future.
> Cheers."

Also, user "baritus" gave his opinion:

> "thanks for the positive article and it's good that people will now know the difference between pre-mined/insta-mined coins and those which are fair."

On the 15th of October, an alpha version of the Digitalcoin Android Wallet App was released on the Google Play Store. Praise was given to Ahmed (from the Digitalcoin IRC Freenode Chatroom) who had created it. However, a few issues with the code (connecting to nodes) later emerged since version one of the wallet client had been available. Work was underway to resolve this.

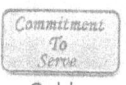

Gold

Antique Gold

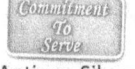

Antique Silver

Silver

On the 19th of October at 02:03 UTC, official Digitalcoin forum user "MobGod" submitted a thread titled "Coin". He wanted to find out how interested the community was concerning the design and manufacture of physical metal Digitalcoins of 1.5 inches in diameter. Eight different metal options were advertised. These are shown in the image on the right:

Black Nickel

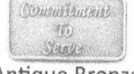

Antique Bronze

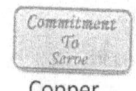

Copper

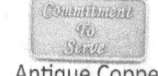

Antique Copper

On the 30th of October at 01:47:43 UTC, user "BitcoinFX" said:

> "I'm pleased to announce that I've successfully added the digitalcoin - Portable USB project to indiegogo.com
>
> See: http://igg.me/at/digitalcoin-usb/x/5215693
>
> Backing for the project ends 32 days from today on Sat. 30th November 2013.
>
> Please tell your family, friends and co-workers. Tweet about it, blog about it and/or anything else you can think of to promote the project and to further support digitalcoin.
>
> Any questions, comments or suggestions please send me a PM (preferably via the digitalcoin forum).
>
> digitalcoin forum topic: http://digitalcoin.co/forums/index.php/topic,203.0.html
>
> Thank you for your support."

Other events which occurred in the month of October were:

- On the 10th of October, the last auction for shares in CryptoAve began.

- On the 17th of October, 400 shares in CryptoAve were still available.

- On the 22nd of October, user "BitcoinFX" was pleased to announce that he had successfully submitted the "Digitalcoin - Portable USB Project" on www.indiegogo.com (also see comment above in which he advertised the promotion again). Scheduled to end on the 30th of November 2013, it was a means to promote the project to a wider audience.

- On the 26th of October at 13:39:46 UTC, a total of 10,000,000 DGC had been mined/generated up to and including block number 505,400.

- On the 30th of October, there was an update from user "baritus". He expected "closed beta testing" of CryptoAve to commence in late November. This would involve a chosen number of selected individuals as testers. Afterwards, open beta testing would happen.

VERSION ONE WALLET CLIENT RELEASE
SUCCESSFUL

NOVEMBER 2013

I.   Fixed Android Wallet App released on the Google Play Store.

II.   Block reward reduced from 20 DGC to 15 DGC.

III.   Difficulty re-targeting period reduced from 1,080 to 108 blocks.

IV.   Ten community members selected for closed beta testing of CryptoAve.

V.   Market cap went above $1,000,000 for the first ever time.

On the second day of the month, user "Bitcoin.Greece" praised user "ahmed_bodi" after he had fixed the DGC Android Wallet App. He donated 100 DGC as gratitude. On the same day at 02:50:19 UTC, user "ahmed_bodi" said:

"DGC Android Wallet Released and fully working!
https://play.google.com/store/apps/details?id=de.schildbach.wallet.digitalcoin&hl=en
Im always in #digitalcoin and #crypto-expert on freenode for support

However please note exchange rates in the wallet do not working i am in the process of fixing it. after this i am retiring maintaining the code since i would rather switch to electrum and make a litewallet and android wallet at the same time

Donations welcome @ D6tdmDCUkZEUaUyLx4dhZH992yTEJSL1tU or can be done inapp using the tip/donate button"

On the 4th of November at 15:08 UTC, in addition to the "Digitalcoin - Portable USB Project" created on Indiegogo, user "BitcoinFX" posted the following:

"Please support the digitalcoin USB - Thunderclap.it -See: http://thndr.it/1aVQ4gR

We need 100+ supporters via twitter or facebook or tumblr to get the message heard !

If we reach this target the following message will be posted across the supporters accounts on Nov 23, 4:00 PM EST.

" Help to generate support for our digitalcoin USB project on indiegogo #digitalcoin #indiegogo #crowdfunding #ReTweet http://thndr.it/18R9ui5 "

This is a very powerful marketing opportunity - not just for the digitalcoin USB project, but for digitalcoin in general.

If you have a website or blog then you can also embed the Thunderclap.it app / widget with the following code:

Thank you for your support!"

On the 5th of November, the anticipated block reward reduction occurred at block number 523,800. From this point forward, the block time was set at forty seconds and the re-targeting period reduced to 108 blocks. A total of 10,367,998 DGC had been generated up to and including block number 523,799.

Block #523,799 (Reward 20 DGC) November 5th 2013 at 05:26:00 AM UTC

Block #523,800 (Reward 15 DGC) November 5th 2013 at 05:25:28 AM UTC

On the same day at 13:06:36 UTC, user "r32godzilla" said:

"The magical DGC block number of 523,800 was passed a short while ago so officially the DGC V1 updates have now started taking effect. Update your client if you haven't already!"

An article was published on the news site http://cryptosource.org titled "Digitalcoin V1 Update Successful" on the 5th of November. Congratulations were given to the development team for the successful hard fork at block number 523,800:

"Early this morning, Digitalcoin block 523,800 came and went and the hard fork went off without a hitch. Digitalcoin has drastically changed its stats in hopes of combating the inflationary issues it was having as well as the issue of the profit seeking pools driving difficulty up and exploiting the low difficulty moments.

The new update brings a lower block reward of 15 instead of 20. The time between blocks has been increased to 40 seconds from 20. The difficulty retargeting will take effect every 108 blocks instead of every 1080. The difficulty adjustment has also been limited to a maximum of 38% in each direction. These are significant canges and should effectively drop the rewards by approx. 60%.

The hopes of this update is that even if a profit seeking pool hops on to the coin, they will only be able to exploit the low difficulty for 108 blocks at a time, and the difficulty won't be able to spike as high as it would when the profit pool leaves. This is very good for the loyal miner as they will be offered more constant rewards and won't miss out on the low difficulty rewards when the profit pools hit. The drop in rewards and the longer block times will also help combat the inflationary issues and make the coin slightly rarer in hopes of deterring people from simply cashing in as soon as they mine to convert back to BTC.

Another thing working in Digitalcoin's favour is the new CryptoAve exchange set to launch by the end of the year. CryptoAve will offer fiat exchange for DGC (along with SRC, ARG, LTC & BTC). Internal testing is set to begin any day now with a closed beta testing phase starting in late November. Open beta testing and public release for CryptoAve looks promising for sometime in December.

Best of luck to the Digitalcoin Team and congrats on the successful update!"

On the 7th of November at 16:27:31 UTC, user "baritus" said:

"I'm going to keep the OP as an information page from now on. digitalcoin.co will now host all the other details.

We've added a lot of merchants at http://digitalcoin.co/spend"

On the 17th of November, the Bitcoin Satoshi value of one unit of DGC account, according to the website www.cryptocoincharts.info, was:

	Price	Low	Open	Close	High	Volume (BTC)
Cryptsy	4,279.5	4,000	4,383	4,176	5,298	9.51774
Vircurex	4,028.5	3,748	3,748	4,309	5,630	0.428816
Crypto Trade	3,026	562	5,490	562	5,490	0.000289681

Data attaining to trading on Coins-e and CoinEx could not be found. As is evident above, the vast majority of trading still existed on Cryptsy. A market capitalisation of about $250,000 was the case on the day.

Also on the 17th of November at 15:20:45 UTC, user "BitcoinFX" reminded members of the community that the "Digitalcoin USB Flash Drive" campaign on Thunderclap (http://thndr.it/1aVQ4gR) had less than one week to go before the deadline date. One hundred supporters were still being sought after.

On the 22nd of November, the following was announced on Facebook:

> "CryptoAve closed beta testing due to start any day now. Approx 10 lucky DGC community members have been selected by Baritus to give it a first test drive! smile emoticon"

On the following day, user "disclaimer201" created a thread on the official DGC forum at https://forum.digitalcoin.co/threads/933-Bitcointalk-thread. He had noticed the lack of activity on the official Digitalcoin Bitcointalk thread. He stressed the importance of sustaining discussion there so as to keep the thread on the first page of the "Announcements (Altcoins)" section. As a result, this would increase the likelihood of users visiting the thread, hence attract new community members. A weekly update about the coin was suggested by user "jt7382" at the same time.

On the 23rd of November, the "USB Flash Drive" campaign on Thunderclap ended at 16:00 EST. Unfortunately, a total of twenty seven supporters (out of 100) pledged their support. As a result, the message could not be sent to a "social reach" of 4,798 people across social media sites such as Facebook and Twitter.

On the following day at 20:56 UTC, user "MobGod" published a preview of six different DGC metal coins which had just been received after being manufactured. These can be seen on page 76. Members of the community would have the opportunity to buy these in December 2013.

On the 25th of November at 00:28:30 UTC, user "disclaimer201" said:

> "DGC now at 8000+ satoshis, market cap looking good, and I saw a peak of over 1 Million in hashing power KH/s today. It is nice to see it go up again, no reason for it to be traded way below value."

On the 25th of November at 16:38:34 UTC, user "baritus" created a new Bitcointalk thread titled "~DigitalCoin~ 5000 DGC Draw $4000+ |{ FREE ENTRY GUESS GAME} December 12 Draw" on which he posted the following:

> "Hello alt-coin community,
>
> To celebrate the recent optimism in alt coin markets, I'm giving away 5000 DGC to a random lucky person.
>
> How to enter: Guess a number between 1 and 5000
>
> How to win:
> The closest person to the number I've safely written down and stored wins.
>
> Contest ends December 12 at midnight forum(UTC) time."

User "golikcoin" won the contest with his guess of 2013. The total prize was sent on the 14th of December. This happened to be the same day on which the all time high market capitulation of the coin was attained.

On the 26th of November, the market capitalisation of Digitalcoin surpassed $1,000,000 for the first time. Below is a table of the BTC Satoshi values of one unit of DGC account on Cryptsy up to and including the last day of the month:

	Price	Low	Open	Close	High	Volume (BTC)
24th Nov	6,429.5	5,120	5,286	7,573	8,463	46.9773
25th Nov	8,683.5	7,125	7,661	9,706	11,500	93.2217
26th Nov	11,292	8,251	9,709	12,875	13,200	68.4948
27th Nov	12,247	10,109	12,884	11,610	13,260	46.9175
28th Nov	10,528	9,000	11,611	9,445	94,000	33.5168
29th Nov	11,398	9,000	9,811	12,985	13,048	36.0899
30th Nov	21,137.5	11,018	12,985	29,290	45,000	181.340

source: www.cryptocoincharts.info

As is evident in the table, there was a sharp increase in the BTC Satoshi value of one unit of DGC account of approximately 300% on the 30th of November. Taking into consideration the fiat value of Bitcoin was also increasing at the same time, the fiat value of Digitalcoin increased by more than 300%.

On the 30th of November at 20:18:45 UTC, user "baritus" said:

"Doing well. 150%+ in the past 24 hours!"

Also on the last day of the month at 23:45:48 UTC, user "disclaimer201" stated the market capitalisation and the value of one unit of DGC account:

16   Digitalcoin, $ 5,332,578, $ 0.48, 11,014,131 DGC, +242.20 %

Other events which occurred in the month of November were:

- Digitalcoin was added to the online wallet service at https://coinwallet.co on the 15th of November.

- On the 15th of November, thanks to J P Buntinx, people could buy PC Steam Game Keys using Digitalcoin as payment http://www.cryptogamekeys.com/.

- For the whole duration of the first year history, the lowest Bitcoin Satoshi value of one unit of DGC account was recorded on the 18th of November. To be specific, the value was 300 BTC Satoshi (would not be lower than this until the 6th of June 2014).

- On the 24th of November, user "baritus" announced that he had been talking to the owners of BTC38 to get Digitalcoin trading there.

- On the 28th of November, user "ShimalH" wanted to design and create a new Digitalcoin Reddit page. However, he was convinced otherwise and became a moderator of the current one.

- On the 30th of November, the "USB Flash Drive" campaign on the website http://igg.me/at/digitalcoin-usb (Indiegogo) came to an end.

- Digitalcoin was added to the site http://coinwik.org/Digitalcoin on the 30th of November. On there, one can find out the basic coin specification, exchanges, mining pools, block explorers etc. of the coin. On the same day, user "baritus" encouraged people to visit http://digiclick.co/?view=home (an advertising platform on which users can earn DGC).

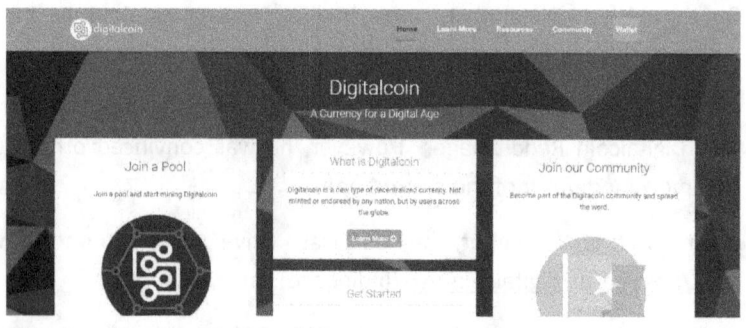

ALL TIME HIGH MARKET CAPITALISATION

DECEMBER 2013

I.   Closed beta testing of CryptoAve (exclusive DGC exchange) began.

II.   Digitalcoin reached an all time high market capitalisation.

III. Version 1.1 of the wallet client released (mandatory).

IV.   DGC/BTC and DGC/CNY markets were added to BTC38 and Bter.

V.   Block number 625,800 reached (11,898,013 DGC mined/generated).

A redesign of the official Digitalcoin website was proposed by user "ShimalH". He had noticed the site provided sufficient information for those who already have knowledge of cryptocurrencies, but not enough information for those who are new to cryptocurrencies. He had been putting together a redesign (see page 84) for the website to make it more user friendly and visually appealing. Some people were happy that efforts were being made to improve the official website, but user "disclaimer201" was quoted as saying:

> "I'm all in for a new webdesign, but this is way too colorful for my taste. It hurts my eyes. Could we tone it down maybe just a tad bit?
>
> The Digitalcoin.co page looks less flashy than say CGB's website or others, but it looks more serious and less distractive."

On the 2nd of December, a status update was posted on Facebook regarding CryptoAve. User "baritus" was still diligently testing the code for bugs/issues. He emphasised that this was not an easy task. He assured the community that closed beta testing was only a few days away. As mentioned previously in November, ten lucky people had already been chosen to test it.

Two days later, an article was published at http://finance.yahoo.com titled "Transact at Five Times the Speed of Bitcoin with Popular Bitcoin Alternative Digitalcoin". Reference was made to "key infrastructure" already in place such as a paper wallet generator, an Android Wallet App and applications for Windows, Mac and Linux. It also stated the three major cryptocurrency exchanges offering DGC trading at the time; these being Cryptsy, Vircurex and Crypto Trade.

On the 5th of December at 01:35:11 UTC, user "Robert Lewandowski" said:

> "When did you guys the USD DGC Exchange would be released?"

User "r32godzilla" replied by saying the following:

> "The exchange is being readied for closed beta testing. Baritus has spent the last week or so bug checking the code and is in the process of getting some servers up for the closed beta. Hopefully the closed testing phase will start in the next day or so. For more information I would join DGC IRC (see my sig) and also the Digitalcoin forum.
>
> Cheers!"

On the 7th of December, closed beta testing of the CryptoAve exchange trading engine finally began. One day prior to this announcement, user "baritus" said the following in the Digitalcoin IRC Chatroom:

> "Okay guys, got everything worked out on server. Beta 100% sure tomorrow, we'll be testing the code and UI."

On the 8th of December at 05:27:54 UTC, user "disclaimer201" said:

"Newsflash:

CryptoAve is currently in closed beta-testing, according to the DGC facebook page: https://www.facebook.com/DigitalCoinDGC .

Here is a new *poll* (unofficial) about which coin should be added next to BTC-E: https://bitcointalk.org/index.php?topic=361576.0
If you want it to be DGC you could vote. Of course, even if DGC were to win there is no guarantee BTC-E will add it. Nor am I certain they should. It isn't really needed when CryptoAve launches and DGC would only become another playground for DavidPate, Fontas, and some other super-manipulators over there.

I really like that design for the *new digitalcoin website* presented at the DGC forums. I hope it will go live soon. It's fresh! If you haven't seen it, check it out: http://digitalcoin.co/forums/index.php/topic,265.0.html

Network hashrate is pretty stable, currently at 434.00 M/H, price is just below 20000 satoshis. Un-der-val-ued. Wouldn't be surprised if support for some of these other coins with pre-mines is over soon. DGC belongs in the top 10 category, and this should soon be reflected by its 'market capitalization' as well.

If you still don't know *why you should choose DGC* over other coins check out: http://digitalcoin.co/forums/index.php/topic,286.0.html where we are currently discussing exactly this question."

Also on the 8th of December, user "matt608" made a recommendation to get DGC actively trading on BTC38 (a large cryptocurrency exchange in China).

On the 10th of December at 15:46:25 UTC, user "baritus" posted the following:

"Updates:
1. The network is maintaining a stable hash rate and difficulty.
2. The community is growing at a record breaking pace.
3. CryptoAve is in testing and will go into open beta when ready."

On the 13th of December, user "ShimalH" announced another project he had just embarked upon. Currently being developed at the time, he announced an online marketplace called "Coinmart.co". Initial investors were sought after to help towards the cost of the project. A description of "Coinmart.co" was:

> Coinmart will connect you to buyers from all across the globe wanting to buy your product. Think of it like the Amazon for Cryptocurrencies. As a merchant it will help scale your business without the hassle of mainting your own website. As a service provider it will help connect you with countless potential buyers. As normal guy it will help you sell well just about anything

On the 14th of December at 06:09:49 UTC, user "baritus" said:

> "DGC is now also trading at btc38.com"

Shortly after its addition to BTC38, Digitalcoin began active trading on a second Chinese exchange called Bter.

Besides the addition to BTC38 (English version to be released on the 13th of March 2014) and Bter, the market capitalisation (the USD fiat value of all DGC units of account generated/mined to date) had been surging. As can be seen in the table below, the Bitcoin Satoshi value of one unit of DGC account (on Cryptsy) more than doubled in the space of three days. This surge resulted in the all time high market capitalisation of the coin on the 14th of December 2013. A value of approximately $9,009,788 was attained (at the time of publication of this book, this high has never been surpassed).

	Price	Low	Open	Close	High	Volume (BTC)
11th of Dec	28,604.5	22,222	26,209	31,000	34,000	99.1414
12th of Dec	38,875	30,999	31,000	46,750	48,000	199.212
13th of Dec	51,875	36,750	46,750	57,000	61,000	338.795
14th of Dec	64,796	54,800	57,000	72,592	----	----

source: www.cryptocoincharts.info

On the 17th of December, a video titled "Coinmart Introductory Video" was uploaded to YouTube. By viewing it, the overall message entails how Coinmart can benefit a online business in terms of selling one's product to a wider customer base.

On the 19th of December at 16:08 UTC on the official DGC Forum, user "baritus" announced the following:

"[UPDATE][DGC] DigitalCoin V1.1 Mandatory Update

Hello,

This is a mandatory update for all DigitalCoin users. All wallet QT and daemon users must update before block 625,800. Please update ASAP.

Change log:
- Difficulty stepping further refined to 25% in either direction.
- Checkpoints updated.
- Further library improvements for even more stability. Libraries are now compiled separately and can be shared with SRC and ARG clients.
- Wallet and daemon no longer require any configuration to synchronize. Just download and run.
- Lowered amount of memory used by a running client.

...DOWNLOAD LINKS...

How to Update:
Replace your current wallet files with the ones provided in the download."

One again, on the same day, a corresponding independent new article was written by user "CryptoMaster" at http://cryptosource.org/digitalcoin-v1-1-mandatory-update. Also, on this day, user "ShimalH" announced the following:

"We have decided to sell of 10% of our shares in Coinmart before launch, much in the same way as CryptoAve. Shares give you the right to claim declared dividends. All net income will either go to retained earnings for building reserves, or be declared as dividends and distributed proportionally."

On the 22nd of December at 08:34:21 UTC, user "r32godzilla" said:

> "Yep not long now until CAve is released. We are looking at open beta around 12th of Jan and then CAve to open around 30th of Jan according to Baritus.
>
> Dgc has the dev, community and services to go far, so in time it should overtake all the other coins that lack these services and support.
>
> Roll on dgc!" 😊

On Christmas Day, user "baritus" created a thread on the official Digitalcoin forum as a means to wish everyone a Merry Christmas. He was quoted as saying:

> "Hello Community,
>
> I'd like to take this opportunity to wish every one of you a Merry Christmas and a Happy New Year!
>
> It's been a great 232.782 days together and I'm sure we can accomplish much more.
>
> Regards,
> Baritus (AKA Rudolph)"

On Boxing Day, testing of the trading engine (phase one of closed beta) had been completed. Phase two (testing of the rest of the CryptoAve website) was scheduled to commence on the 6th of January 2014. Thanks were given to all beta testers.

Block #625,800 (Reward 15 DGC) December 30th 2013 at 08:08:08 PM UTC

Coming into effect at this block, the difficulty code adjustments began. No change of the block reward or block time occurred. A reminder was issued to users, who had not yet updated, to do so. A total of 11,898,013 DGC had been mined/ generated up to and including this block.

Other events which occurred in the month of December were:

- On the 2nd of December, user "BitcoinFX" notified the community that the last remaining "15 GB USB Flashdrive Flipcard's - White - printed with the Digitalcoin logo" had just been listed for auction on E-bay.

- On the 6th of December, the number of subscribers at .../r/digitalcoin on Reddit surpassed one hundred.

- A US based online merchandiser called Finite By Design began to stock Digitalcoin USB Flashdrive Flipcards on the 15th of December. They accepted payments in BTC, LTC, PPC, CGB (now CBX), DGC, XPM and PayPal.

- On the 17th of December, a Digitalcoin related marketplace was created at http://reddit.com/r/dgcmarket by user "supermario420".

- On the 18th of December, Digitalcoin was added to the AltcoinTipBot.

- On the 18th of December, user "MobGod" announced the availability of DGC metal coins. Images of three types of coins, besides their corresponding costs, are shown below.

- On the 22nd of December, after the release of version 1.1 of the wallet client, the corresponding Mac OS X client was released.

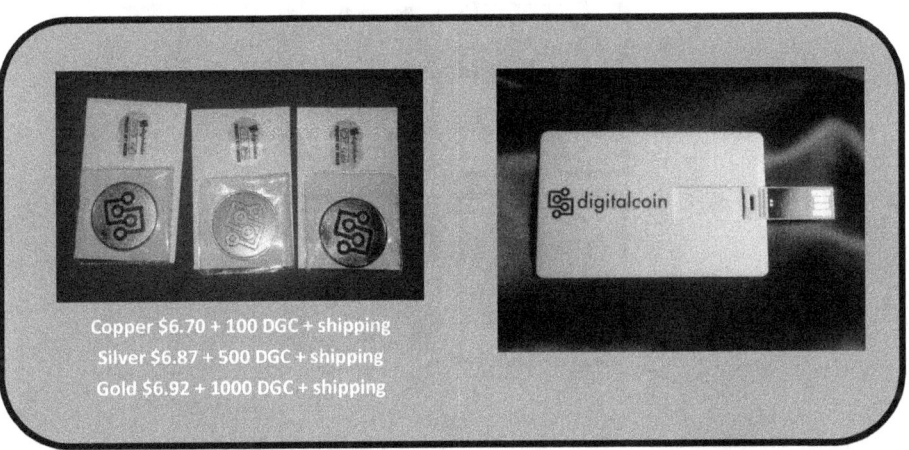

Copper $6.70 + 100 DGC + shipping
Silver $6.87 + 500 DGC + shipping
Gold $6.92 + 1000 DGC + shipping

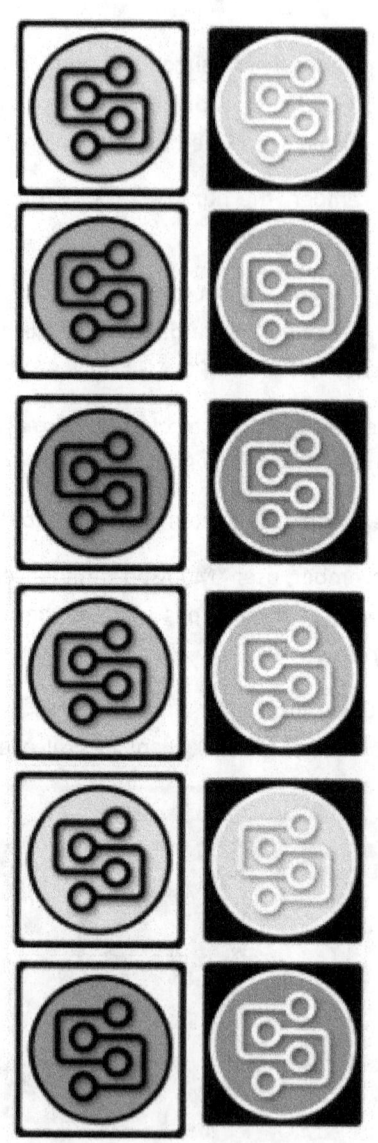

OPEN BETA TESTING OF CRYPTOAVE BEGAN

JANUARY 2014

I.   Users had problems withdrawing Digitalcoin from Cryptsy.

II.   Digitalcoin became the third cryptocurrency added to http://blockr.io.

III. CryptoAve open beta testing began.

IV.   A lightweight wallet client introduced called Dub (Digitalcoin Hub)

V.   FinTech News Website "Follow The Coin" interviewed user "baritus".

Some users of Cryptsy were concerned about not being able to withdraw their DGC holdings from there. Their withdrawals were pending with a related confirmation via e-mail. They reported that other cryptocurrency withdrawals were fine. Perhaps Cryptsy needed to update to the latest version of the wallet client. On the 2nd of January at 18:54:58 UTC, user "baritus" was quoted as saying:

> "There are no issues with the network and it is processing transactions perfectly.
>
> Contact your services for any issues you experience, they most likely need to update their clients to send/receive DGC again."

Many other coins on Cryptsy had experienced similar issues since May 2013.

On the 5th of January, user "bricema" thought DGC should definitely be on BTC-e and was undervalued. He asked whether DGC could hit $1.5 after the launch of CryptoAve. In response, user "baritus" on the same day at 17:20:09 UTC said:

> "We hit $0.80+ without it, so yes, I do believe that is easily achievable.
>
> Updates:
> --------------------
> - DGC will be only the third coin added to http://blockr.io
> - We tested the engine in the first phase closed beta successfully. CryptoAve second phase testing is now in motion.
> The second phase focuses on the supporting services of the exchange.
> - A new DGC website with a focus on ease of use and attracting new users is complete and in the process of being implemented.
> - DGC V1.1 update was a success and we are no longer experiencing fluctuations due to the difficulty highs and lows."

Over the past few days, the block explorer at http://dgc.cryptocoinexplorer.com kept going offline, which led www.coinmarketcap.com to temporarily delist DGC. Members of the community voiced their disappointment. An alternative explorer was sought after which would reduce the risk of the coin being delisted in the future. This became reality on the 7th of January as the anticipated explorer at http://blockr.io added Digitalcoin. On this day at 13:07:30 UTC, user "baritus" said:

> "We now have a block explorer, parser, and data aggregator all in one.
>
> https://dgc.blockr.io/ Enjoy!"

User "disclaimer201" described it as an excellent service. He was also looking forward to the fresh new design of the official Digitalcoin website.

On the 8th of January, J P Buntinx wrote an article titled "Digitalcoin Is On The Move!". Published on the website "Digital Money Times", he described how the value of altcoins had been decreasing over the past few days. This coincided with an increase in the USD value of one Bitcoin. However, on the 8th of January, the value of Digitalcoin increased by approximately 25%. He cited the large daily trade volume (3.1 million DGC) over the preceding 24 hours on the Chinese exchange BTC38 as the most probable cause for this. J P Buntinx ended the article by saying:

"Is this a sign of things to come? Could it be just a one-off? All we know is that, at the end of this month, the CryptoAve exchange will launch, *where you will be able to trade Digitalcoin , as well as Securecoin and Argentum, against fiat currency*, which will make it a lot easier for many people to start getting involved with Cryptocurrency."

Four days later, open beta (all members of the community permitted) testing of the upcoming CryptoAve exchange began. Again, an article was written by J P Buntinx who wrote it just before open beta was scheduled to begin. Users were told they had to e-mail user "baritus" in order to gain open beta access. Many people were eagerly awaiting the final full release of CryptoAve at the end of January.

On the 18th of January at 14:57 UTC, user "coinnoisseur" proposed an alternative design to the Digitalcoin Paper Wallet. He advised people to become informed about how to take the necessary security measures. He said the following:

"All you have to do is create a personal and a private key and the QR-codes. Place them on the design and print."

During the first week of open beta testing, there were a couple of times when the site http://cryptoave.com/beta was unavailable to those who were permitted to login. These were instances of the code being updated after constructive feedback had been submitted to user "baritus". On the 20th of January, user "baritus" posted his first tweet (@OfficialBaritus) which read:

> "First tweet: CryptoAve open beta is coming on nicely with updates currently taking place. Thank you to all the testers."

On the 26th of January at 13:06 UTC, user "ShimalH" announced yet another project he had been working on. It was a lightweight (no requirement to fully download the whole blockchain) Digitalcoin wallet client based upon MultiBit called Dub (short for Digitalcoin Hub). He got the idea for it (a side project) before he began work on Coinmart. Three "quick facts" were listed at the time:

> "Dub is the first lightweight wallet that supports a cryptocurrency other than Bitcoin;
>
> No other cryptocurrency, not even Litecoin, has a lightweight wallet;
>
> The platform which it runs on, digitalcoinj, is only the third Java implementation of a cryptocurrency's protocol after Bitcoin and Litecoin."

A LIGHTWEIGHT DIGITALCOIN WALLET

Corresponding download links for the Java implementation were posted for users to test it and report any bugs/faults. User "ShimalH" said Coinmart would eventually be integrated with Dub allowing people to purchase items directly from the wallet. As a means to facilitate this feature, the launch of Coinmart was pushed forward to the 1st of March 2014. He had also contacted external developers for help. Future plans were a decentralised exchange, a lotto site and a mining pool.

On the 27th of January, an interview was published by "Follow The Coin". The interviewer questioned user "baritus" about Digitalcoin, Securecoin, Argentum and CryptoAve. The full transcript can be found in the appendix of this book.

CryptoAve open beta testing was still ongoing as the month came to a close. User "r32godzilla" gave his opinion on the 30th of January at 02:46:42 UTC. He was quoted as saying:

"Yes I think there is a very good chance DGC will get a nice boost once CryptoAve opens especially with dgc to USD and the option to use dgc to buy CAve shares.

I like the name digitalcoin as it is now currently. Renaming it to digicoin etc is a bit similar to coins like digibytes etc. Digitalcoin is a great name. Digital technology is regarded as the pinnacle pretty much these days so it makes sense to have a coin called Digitalcoin that is used electronically as a cryptocurrency.

With all the hard work going on behind the scenes and continual development of great and usable services hopefully that helps make 2014 the year of Digitalcoin and we see it move into the upper echelon of Cryptocurrency."

Other events which occurred in the month of January were:

- On the 20th of January, user "Hazard" created the first DGC dice game.

- On the 27th of January, user "coinnoisseur" created colour DGC logos which were made freely available for anyone wishing to promote DGC (page 92).

- User "kenel" organised and promoted about three poker tournaments during the month. There was a signup fee of 100 DGC and grand prize of 1,500 DGC. Another one was scheduled for the 1st of February 2014.

CRYPTOAVE EXCHANGE TESTED, IMPLEMENTED AND LAUNCHED

FEBRUARY 2014

I.   Versions 0.1 and 0.1.1 of Dub (lightweight wallet client) released.

II. Security of the official Digitalcoin forum increased after it was attacked.

III. Five minor cryptocurrency exchanges added DGC throughout the month.

IV. CryptoAve exchange launched on the 21st of February.

V.   A new alternative and official Digitalcoin logo unveiled.

On the first day of the month, an update (version 0.1) to Dub (the first lightweight desktop client for Digitalcoin announced last month) was released. At 20:39 UTC on the official Digitalcoin forum, user "ShimalH" was quoted as saying:

> "Some of you may have downloaded the test version of Dub, called MultiDGC. Basically that was Dub without the front-end design. As of now Dub is fully functional with the front-end design and is release ready. There are a few tiny UI tweaks which we will implement in version 0.2 which we will release next Saturday.
> A dedicated website will also be put up for Dub in the coming weeks."

Download links for version 0.1 were made available for Windows, Mac and Linux users. As was the case the previous month, user "ShimalH" wanted users to tell him if they found any bugs or errors.

Also on the 1st of February, user "baritus" had welcoming news about the upcoming CryptoAve exchange. A revised launch date of the 10th of February was announced, pending some legal documents due on the 8th of February.

On the following day, user "baritus" wanted help to select a new Digitalcoin logo design primarily for the revamped official website. Some design proposals had already been submitted:

A specific forum thread was created to discuss the above submissions. It would not be until the 27th of February that a brand new logo was unveiled.

On the 4th of February at 13:42:17 UTC, user "baritus" said:

"Here is a list of some of the development happening right now:

Developer: baritus
Projects: CryptoAve Currency Exchange (Open Beta Complete), DGC Website Redesign, DGC Text Based MMO

Developer: ShimalH
Projects: Dub DGC lightweight wallet (Beta Released), CoinMart Auctions and Marketplace

Developer: clapyohands & ahmedbodi
Projects: TBA Application

Developer: rawdawg & clapyohands
Projects: DGC Multi-user Poker Platform

Source: http://digitalcoin.co/forums/index.php/topic,819.0.html"

In response to the update of current ongoing developments, two members of the community said the following. Firstly, user "disclaimer201" said:

"Love how you always strive to implement suggestions of the community. It makes DGC a truly decentralized and democratic project. CryptoAve Beta looks very professional as well."

Secondly, user "r32godzilla" said:

"Thats a great list of projects in development. DGC really is a solid coin to get behind and put in your cryptocoin portfolio. We are starting to get a very good team together now and it will be very interesting to see how it grows in the coming months and years.

Can't wait for Feb 10!"

On the 7th of February at 04:40:01 UTC, user "disclaimer201" notified the community that Digitalcoin was ranked 16th in terms of mineable cryptocurrencies.

Over the past several days, the official Digitalcoin forum had been unavailable due to issues with the local server on which it existed. On the 8th of February at 16:54:47 UTC, user "baritus" said:

> "Forum is back and it has been improved."

The forum had experienced some kind of spam attack which corrupted the database. As a result, user "baritus" had to rebuild the database, update the forum infrastructure and add security patches to reduce the risk of it recurring. As a bonus, the forum started to function more efficiently.

Members of the community were eagerly awaiting the release of CryptoAve. It was scheduled to go live on the 10th of February. Some were puzzled why the value of Digitalcoin was not increasing in anticipation of this event. The value of Bitcoin was crashing on Mt Gox (infamous BTC exchange) at the time. This had the effect of pulling the value of DGC down as well as those of many other cryptocurrencies.

On the 9th of February at 08:58:46 UTC, user "ShimalH" said:

> "Hi all
>
> I've released v0.1.1 of Dub. This version is mainly for bug fixes. We are still working on more features which include an Integrated Miner and P2P pool so stay tuned
>
> You can read more info about Dub in the announcement thread here :
> http://digitalcoin.co/forums/index.php/topic,773.0.html
>
> Download Links View download links here :
> http://digitalcoin.co/forums/index.php/topic,824.0.html
>
> Changelog: Minor UI Tweaks; Fixed Currency Ticker; Fixed Language Issues;
>
> Added an automatic updater to Dub"

Unfortunately, on the 10th of February, the scheduled launch of CryptoAve did not go ahead. A decision was made to postpone it in light of the recent events over at Mt Gox and a couple of legal documents yet to be received. A tentative launch date of the 14th of February was put forward. On the same day at 22:29:03 UTC, user "disclaimer201" said:

> "Given today's Gox security drama this was the only logical decision. We don't want to remember CryptoAve's opening to coincide with the worst day for crypto in years. Let the situation calm down a bit. A few more days more or less of waiting time won't make a big difference. Speculators are gonna do with the DGC price what they wish anyhow for now. Let them. Won't stop DGC having a bright future."

Yet again, user "baritus" thanked everyone for their patience.

Four days later, the launch of CryptoAve still remained on hold due to the BTC exchange DDOS attacks at Mt Gox and the malleability issues evident there. User "baritus" was working hard to fix this issue for CryptoAve and so make it more secure and resilient to attack. There was a chance of the launch going ahead in the next few days depending on progress made.

On the 15th of February at 14:58:07 UTC, user "baritus" said:

> "No one cares about the success of DGC and CryptoAve more than I do. I am the largest stakeholder in both and believe me all decisions are made for the best interest of DGC and C.Ave (since my interests are directly correlated).
>
> As a rational holder, I will not launch CryptoAve when the most important network for its success is experiencing attacks(BTC). I believe that I have a working solution for the transaction malleability. I am implementing and testing it. Everything else is ready to go, including the custom built software which has been tested in both Closed and Open Betas."

About one hour later, user "baritus" announced on Twitter (@OfficialBaritus) that he had found a malleability fix. As soon as he had tested and implemented it, he was confident of the release of CryptoAve soon thereafter.

On the 17th of February at 14:21:15 UTC, user "baritus" said:

> "Hello,
>
> I've completed a fix for BTC processing and we're back on track. I'm now applying that fix across all currencies and testing the processing before launch.
>
> Official Launch Date: February 21
>
> This is a confirmed date. Launch will be on this date regardless of any developments."

On the following day, an exchange called PmToCoins announced that the trading pair DGC/BTC had been recently added to their platform. They assured users of quick support via Twitter (@pmtocoins) and Skype. Digitalcoin experienced negligible trading activity there. Besides that addition, there were other very minor exchanges which initiated trading of the coin throughout the month. These were:

Exchange	Date Added
Bitchanger	10/02/2014
Cryptorush	10/02/2014
OpenEx	18/02/2014
CryptoAltex	24/02/2014

One day before the launch of CryptoAve, user "disclaimer201" created a promotional giveaway on Bitcointalk. It was described as a "No strings attached" giveaway which gave 5 DGC to the first 100 people who posted their wallet address.

On the 21st of February, the launch occurred. To be specific, it was announced to the community on the following day (UTC). On Reddit, it was announced at 02:09:04 UTC. Slightly later, on the 22nd of February at 02:51:25 UTC, user "r32godzilla" posted an announcement on the official DGC Bitcointalk thread (first) that https://www.cryptoave.com is open.

On the 23rd of February at 11:56:59 UTC, user "disclaimer201" said:

> "Congrats to the opening of CryptoAve! Lot's of work is still to be done of course.
>
> I'm looking forward to the new website so that new users get a better impression about the coin and will be willing to mine it or invest in it."

On the 24th of February, the community were made aware that Digitalcoin would be represented by Andrew Davidson at the upcoming Cryptocurrency Convention in New York City. This announcement was made one day after user "CoinBuzz" had recommended the coin should send someone there to speak.

Three days later, a new design of the Digitalcoin logo was unveiled. It was the result of weeks of discussion and participation from devoted designers:

On the last day of the month, user "scorpty" on the official DGC forum enquired why Digitalcoin was not on https://www.mintpal.com/voting. In less than 24 hours, after a suggested coin submission by user "fmg", the coin was ready to be voted for. A community effort followed to drive addition onto the cryptocurrency exchange called Mintpal.

Also on the 28th of February, it was reported that Mt Gox had gone bankrupt.

VERSION (CORE) 2.0 WALLET CLIENT ANNOUNCED

MARCH 2014

I.   Digitalcoin Foundation initial formation announced.

II.   A dedicated Digitalcoin TipBot on Reddit went live.

III.   For the first time, USD trading began on CryptoAve and Prelude (by Moolah).

IV.   Version 2.0 (Core) of the wallet client announced.

V.   An updated official Digitalcoin website went live.

Towards the end of January 2014, user "ShimalH" pushed forward the launch of Coinmart to the first day of March. Unfortunately, it was postponed indefinitely due to recent flaws pointed out in custom Bitcoin wallets. A professional security team were needed to review Coinmart. He went onto say:

> "The security team which we will be working have given us a time frame of roughly 2-3 weeks to identify security flaws, if any, and to fix them. Despite this we have finished all of the back-end development, its just the front-end now that needs a little polishing up before launch."

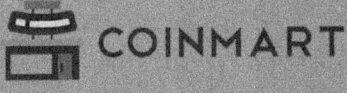

On the 1st of March at 22:27:04 UTC, user "baritus" answered questions put forward by user "Xmansk" two days previously. These were:

When will new DGC website design be online?
New DGC design will be up when it's completed and tested. It's currently in advanced development stage, I estimate a week to two.

When will marketing campaign start?
Marketing campaign will start with the new site opening and USD on CryptoAve(within days).

Will marketing campaign target media like Coindesk?
Marketing campaign will target media and also will include paid advertising on many crypto related websites.

Who is Andrew Davidson who will speak about DGC at http://cryptocurrencyconvention.com/ ?
Andrew Davidson is known as rawdawg in IRC, he's in there often.

Do you agree that marketing is now number 1 priority?
Marketing is number one priority, hence the redesign of DGC website, new logo, and marketing push.

Will DGC join this event http://www.coinsumm.it/ ?
Not sure of that summit, we will be at the other for sure.

Will CAve accept SEPA?
Maybe in the future, C Ave will accept SEPA, but not for a while.

What do you think about current DGC price development?
DGC price is following the same trend as the market, although I think it shouldn't be. Not many have dedicated exchanges and the same development that DGC is getting.

On the 2nd of March, user "rawdawg" announced the formation of a Digitalcoin Foundation to further promote and enhance the coin. Its aim was for it to be a representative organisation in which transparency was upheld. It would also serve as the primary news outlet for the community. At present, the website at http://www.dgcfoundation.com no longer exists.

At the time, the mission statement of the Digitalcoin Foundation was:

> "To educate the general public on the many features Digitalcoin has to offer, including security, speed, continuing development, and consistency. With zero successful blockchain forks and multiple updates we believe that once the public is introduced to what we have to offer, the information will do the rest. We will not rest until Digitalcoin is on top!"

On the 4th of March, there were proposals to update the code base. A lower block re-target time of eight blocks (approximately every 5 mins) was being considered.

Also on this day, a new Digitalcoin TipBot was launched. Running initially on a dedicated computer by /r/digitalcoin moderator /u/ThinkThrough, it allows people to send/receive certain amounts of DGC on Reddit. It was forked from the well-known and popular /r/altcointip source code. The normal tipping syntax applies:

> +/u/dgctipbot [@user|ADDRESS] [$|€|R|¥|£][AMOUNT|KEYWORD]
> [dgc|digitalcoin|digitalcoins|Ð]

Two days later, USD verifications began on CryptoAve (trading against USD was activated a few days later). User "baritus" asked the community which additional crypto they wanted to see alongside BTC, DGC, LTC, SRC, ARG and PPC.

On the 10th of March, after CryptoAve had been offline for a couple of days, some maintenance had been completed. Some problems, which were specific for some users, had been fixed (deposits/withdrawals). Hacking attempts had also been evident. Three days later at 12:36:03 UTC, user "baritus" said:

> "Hello, Thanks. Yes, the security system I put in is heavily focused on the trading and withdrawal/transfer/deposit code. It's all tweaked and running smooth now.
>
> Once all of CryptoAve's features are enabled and we can be confident on all fronts, you'll see tremendous growth. For now, I prefer slower growth that allows the site to improve and evolve along with it. I'm not a fan of meteoric rises leading to crashes, I prefer being prepared so when the rise comes, it's properly supported by fundamentals and services."

On the 14th of March at 23:13:57 UTC, Reddit user "/u/ThinkThrough" posted the first "Bi-weekly Digitalcoin News Thread". Contained within, he broadcasted the latest events related to Digitalcoin. Topics touched upon concerned the recently released tipbot, the theft of DGC from user "baritus", the auctioning of shares in the upcoming marketplace called Coinmart.co and other stories. Help was requested to push DGC onto the exchange sites Poloniex and Vault of Satoshi.

On the 18th of March, user "baritus" released an update regarding the security recoding of CryptoAve (shutdown for two days). Once again, the exchange had been offline due to worse than expected hacking attempts. This was an opportunity for the developers to bolster its security. He emphasised that no coins had been stolen. Furthermore, a cash injection had just been received for hiring an additional software engineer for the exchange. A few hours later, one was hired.

Since the new Digitalcoin logo was unveiled, designers were eager to utilise and incorporate it into improving the coin's image. One of these projects was by user "teillagory" who redesigned the opening post of the official Digitalcoin Bitcointalk thread. His design set out clearly general information, including exchanges, pools and services of the coin, therefore making it all more accessible. A lot of praise and congratulations were given for his work. Another project was by user "transcoder" who designed the Digitalcoin paper wallet as shown below (middle). He gave credit to Canton Becker for the original tri-fold template.

On the 21st of March an exchange called Prelude (by Moolah) initiated live USD deposits and withdrawals (account verification too). Users were promised trading of DGC/USD would begin in four days time (25/03/2014 9 AM EST). On the 17th of March, the trading pair DGC/BTC went live. Prelude no longer exists.

On the 23rd of March at 05:39:53 UTC, user "disclaimer201" said:

"DGC V1.2 will be an important issue as the loyal miner base of DGC has gone down to only 100 Mhash due to the latest Multipool "attacks" and overall price loss of Bitcoin and DGC.

DGC V1.2 should be brought on its way asap or we might see veeeeeeery long blocks. Average block time already is up to 3 minutes instead of the 40 second target after the last exploit from multipools. If the update isn't done before either more loyal miners pick DGC back up again, it might be possible that the block times go up even more until the point that you can neither use DGC as intended, or worse - not use it at all anymore, and even have difficulties reaching new blocks before you could set up a difficulty adjustment. One recent example: MoonCoin has just barely survived (considerably worse) attacks by multipools than dgc as it didn't have a multipool-countering mechanism in effect as DGC has right now. At one point it took half a day or longer for a single block to be found. Multipools had skyrocketed the difficulty so much that none of the loyal miners wanted to mine anymore. It took over a week to even get to a relatively close block when the intended update fork set in and miners were basically mining the blocks for free until then.

I know lots of stuff is going on, but we should make this issue a priority as you want to give everyone some time to update their clients."

Also on the 23rd of March at 18:14:29 UTC, user "baritus" said:

"Updates:
- New DGC site is ready and live at http://digitalcoin.co.
- DGC 2.0 Core update has been announced. It brings Kimoto Gravity Well difficulty adjustment as well as a code base update."

Two days later, an Android wallet app was released on the Google Play Store. A few days previously, "Hash Engineering Solutions" had taken over its development.

On the 26th of March at 12:29:06 UTC, user "baritus" said:

"I am going to use a custom difficulty algorithm in the upcoming 2.0 update. It is yet to be named. "

After initially deciding to adopt the Kimoto Gravity Well Difficulty Re-targeting Algorithm (derived from Megacoin), a technical discussion ensued about how the code could be improved upon to best suit Digitalcoin. User "r32godzilla" thought it was another example of how unique and innovative the developers were being. On the 26th of March at 23:38:11 UTC, user "Samson" posted the following:

"It's not about allowing people to mine more DGC in less time, quite the opposite. It will prevent multipools from hopping on and grabbing all the coins quickly until the difficulty raises and then leaving until it drops down again.

Here's some info from #digitalcoin today :

[26/03 19:23] <@baritus> finished work on a new difficulty algo
[26/03 19:24] <@samson_> New difficulty algo ?
[26/03 19:24] <@baritus> works way better than KGW at keeping multipools at bay
[26/03 19:24] <@samson_> Ah I see, similar to KGW or completely different ?
[26/03 19:24] <@baritus> completely different
[26/03 19:25] <@baritus> not sure what to name this yet
[26/03 19:34] <@samson_> How does this new algorithm work and any idea when it will be implemented ? I guess this is going in the new v2 release mentioned on the forum in place of KGW.
[26/03 19:35] <@baritus> I don't want to post too much on it, so it doesn't popup somewhere else before I release it

See : Innovation"

On the 28th of March, a Reddit Wiki (Wikipedia) had been added to the official Reddit page of Digitalcoin. The founder of the supplementary resource was looking for suggestions in order to improve its content. At present, the subtitles on the site at https://www.reddit.com/r/digitalcoin/wiki/index are:

All About Cryptocurrencies
All About Digitalcoin
Digitalcoin on Reddit
Services
Utilities

During the month, the Bitcoin Satoshi value of one unit of DGC account had been decreasing. Below is a table of values derived from the exchange called Cryptsy:

	Price	Low	Open	Close	High	Volume (BTC)
1st March	17,524.5	16,141	18,599	16,450	18,790	9.47934
8th March	11,265.5	2,560	12,801	9,730	13,984	45.2546
15th March	9,084.5	7,835	9,279	8,890	9,476	7.44299
22nd March	6,907	4,297	6,809	7,005	7,559	3.22290
29th March	6,180	6,060	6,060	6,300	6,370	2.16186
31st March	6,600.5	5,931	6,201	7,000	7,000	7.68040

source: www.cryptocoincharts.info

Other events which occurred in the month of March were:

- On the 1st of March, the official website was down until server migration was complete. On the same day, the website was back up and running properly.

- The total number of subscribers to the subreddit .../r/digitalcoin surpassed 500 for the first time on the 7th of March

- On the 9th of March, user "baritus" notified the community that roughly 560,000 DGC had been stolen from him. An ex-employee had copied the wallet file and key logged the password from the work computer. He did not let this mishap demotivate his dedication to the Digitalcoin Project. As is evident in the table above, a low of 2,560 BTC Satoshi was reached.

- Also on the 9th of March, the second auction of Coinmart shares began.

- On the 21st of March, several Digitalcoin wallpapers were designed and published (see page 106) as part of a contest initiated by Reddit user "FullMetalGurren". He was willing to give 5 DGC to the best three designs.

ANDREW DAVIDSON SPOKE AT THE FIRST CRYPTOCURRENCY CONVENTION IN NEW YORK

APRIL 2014

I.   Digitalcoin added to the website http://bravenewcoin.com.

II.   Andrew Davidson spoke at the first cryptocurrency convention in NYC.

III.   Digitalcoin announced as ready for active trading on Vault of Satoshi.

IV.   Digitalcoin added to the website http://coingecko.com/en.

V.   Digitalcoin began active trading on the Swaphole exchange.

Since the 4th of March, the Digitalcoin Tipbot had been successful. Users who had generously tipped DGC so far included "/u/FullMetalGurren", "/u/happyfocker", "/u/earthmoonsun" and "/u/techbytes1". On the 2nd of April at 14:36:21 UTC, DGC Tipbot Operator "/u/ThinkThrough" had the following news:

"As some of you may know, I'm running the dgctipbot from a home server. Ongoing electrical work will be performed on the nearby power grid over the following weeks. I thought that I could maintain dgctipbot throughout this period, but the server suffered yet another power outage this morning. Since I want to provide you guys with near 100% uptime, I will be migrating the dgctipbot over to a dedicated VM. The migration should go unnoticed, but be warned that you could experience some delays in tipping/withdraw/deposit if you interact with the bot tonight."

On the 8th of April, user "r32godzilla" anticipated the release of version 2.0 (Core) of the wallet client. He went on to say:

> "Apparently the 2.0 core update is on hold pending more evaluation on the algorithm before it gets released. CryptoAve enhanced website will undergo new testing in 2.5 weeks according to Baritus. Other changes for it in the pipeline as well. Looking forward to seeing it back up and running soon! Approx by May 1st."

On the 9th of April at 13:23:47 UTC, user "baritus" said:

> "Hello, The source of attacks on CryptoAve has now been identified. The vulnerabilities created by the heartbleed bug are exactly what was exploited in an attempt to steal user funds.
>
> CryptoAve itself has never been compromised and it is likely that development will speed up now that we no longer have to worry about solving an exploit that never existed in our code.
>
> The exchange will be back soon. We will have a stronger infrastructure and bank level security.
>
> In closing: CryptoAve was never compromised, it was shut down as a precaution and to strengthen defences. We now know the bug that was causing issues is due to the OpenSSL bug and not any of the code or programming language. Regards, Baritus"

About ten minutes later, user "r32godzilla" congratulated user "baritus" for getting CryptoAve offline in next to no time. The HeartBleed Bug exploit looked to be more widespread than people realised. It effected many other exchanges.

Also on the 9th of April, DGC was added to the website http://bravenewcoin.com. They are described as "A data and research company focused on the blockchain and digital equities industry". A vast array of historical charts, coin specifications and news articles can be found there. By viewing the historical chart of Digitalcoin, the highest USD fiat value of one unit of DGC account was on the 16th of April 2013 at approximately $0.0518 (this value has never been surpassed since then).

On the 9th of April, Andrew Davidson (also known as user "rawdawg") gave a speech at the Scholastic Auditorium in New York City. Remembered as the first cryptocurrency convention, he described DGC as a dedicated, democratic and driven community whose purpose, amongst others, was to sustain its longevity in the crypto space. During the eight minute speech, he also mentioned the exclusive exchange called CryptoAve ("Cryptocurrency Avenue"). A similar amount of time was spent answering questions from the audience. A photo was taken at the event:

On the following day, an exchange based in Canada called Vault of Satoshi announced they had added DGC to their platform. Live trading between DGC and BTC/USD/CAD was promised at a later date. At this point, it was in a state of "penetration" testing. It eventually opened publicly on the 7th of October 2013.

VoS stayed open until the 5th of January 2015 after which no further trades or deposits could be made. However, users were allowed to withdraw DGC until it fully closed its doors on the 5th of February 2015. Mike Curry, the co-founder of VoS, pointed out a new venture the business had shifted focus to.

On the 15th of April, there was a surge in the value of one unit of DGC account as well as the market capitalisation. Values derived from Cryptsy were:

	Price	Low	Open	Close	High	Volume (BTC)
13th April	6,190.5	6,041	6,253	6,128	6,747	6.89443
14th April	6,611	6,109	6,213	7,009	7,175	11.0688
15th April	8,519.5	6,700	7,011	10,028	10,765	29.6029
16th April	9,626.5	8,000	10,030	9,223	12,000	17.3448

source: www.cryptocoincharts.info

On the 15th of April at 11:29:44 UTC, user "baritus" said:

"DGC is a leveraged trade on BTC. When BTC rises, we spike. The way markets have set themselves up, BTC rising is the best fundamental for us."

On the 26th of April at 17:15:09 UTC, user "Tsquared" posted his first comment on the official (first) DGC Bitcointalk thread. He said:

"I can appreciate your wanting to expose someone who lies and manipulates supporters, if that's really what baritus has done. Likewise it would be admirable if you genuinely care that people may have been taken advantage of, but is manipulating this coin severely and hurting all these same people even worse the best way to prove your point?

I for one am very new to crypto currency, and I dumped a few thousand dollars into different ones. BTC and DGC being the ones I have the most into. If I had done more research and seen all the controversy earlier I may not have gone so deep with DGC, but it is what it is and now I have little choice but to hold and hope my investment doesn't get wiped out completely.

It's little guys like me that will be hurt most if you really do kill this coin. Don't know if it matters, just giving my 2 cents, which it seems like is more than my DGC holdings will be worth in the near future. TT"

On the 25th of April at 21:29:05 UTC, Reddit user "/u/ThinkThrough" published the fourth "Bi-weekly Digitalcoin News Thread" in which he discussed issues concerning the cessation of the HeartBleed Bug scare.

On the 26th of April at 18:22:05 UTC, user "baritus" said:

> "Updates:
>
> 1. CryptoAve is coming back online soon! We're also going to have a bounty for any issues found during the testing period.
> 2. DGC 2.0 is complete, but there is one last crashing bug that seems to happen at random blocks. I will be posting the source shortly if I can't solve it.
>
> Thanks!
>
> Baritus"

As the month of April came to a close, work continued on the development of version 2.0 of the wallet client. A difficulty re-targeting algorithm derived from, but not solely the Kimoto Gravity Well, was being constructed and tested.

Other events which occurred in the month of April were:

- On the 8th of April, a new revised version of the official website at http://digitalcoin.co went live thanks to user "baritus".

- On the 13th of April, DGC was added to https://coingecko.com/en. It is a site that ranks many cryptocurrencies according to social, developer and trading activity.

- Thirteen days after the event, the video of Andrew's speech was uploaded at http://www.youtube.com/watch?v=BkBZIilyP2g&feature=youtu.be

- On the 26th of April, the dgc.scryptmining.com mining pool closed. It had been active just after the launch of the coin.

- On the 27th of April, DGC was added to an exchange called Swaphole at https://www.swaphole.com/#!market/DGC/BTC.

ONE YEAR ANNIVERSARY OF DIGITALCOIN

MAY 2014

I.   Digitalcoin Foundation Survey created.

II.   The highest number of subscribers to …/r/digitalcoin reached.

III.   CryptoAve back after being temporarily offline for about one month.

IV.   Coinmart online marketplace released.

V.   Last block of the first year timestamped at block number 856,902.

On the first day of the month, user "DGCBread" (on the official Digitalcoin website) proposed a new generic cryptocurrency forum on which "serious" coins could be discussed. He said it was time coins such as Digitalcoin "break away from underneath the "Bitcoin" umbrella". User "baritus" agreed on any efforts to differentiate DGC from other coins, but Bitcointalk had become the "go to spot". On the 1st of May at 23:57:00 UTC, user "baritus" said:

> "Digitalcoin Facebook site has been updated. If your interested in Digitalcoin please add your like and tell anyone else who might be interested in keeping up to date with DGC news!
>
> https://www.facebook.com/DigitalCoinDGC
>
> Cheers!"

On the 2nd of May, user "kenel" created a "Digitalcoin Foundation Survey" at:

https://www.surveymonkey.com/s/MCSFBTC

He politely asked members of the official forum to complete it (first 20 contributors received 100 DGC each). A better understanding of the community was being sought after. He also wanted to use the information to attract new supporters. The survey included questions relating to gender, age, job, education and so on.

Five days later, the number of subscribers to the official DGC subreddit peaked at 572. At the time of publication of this book, this number has never been surpassed.

On the 8th of May 21:04:20 UTC, user "baritus" said:

"https://www.CryptoAve.Com is live!

If you had shares, register with the same email you had."

On the following day, J P Buntinx wrote yet another article related to CryptoAve. Titled "CryptoAve Exchange Back In Business", he described that the exchange had opened its doors again for users to trade after the failed hacking attempts to steal funds. Users had to, however, register again with their old account username and password. Those users who did this, automatically received their holdings back. CryptoAve would stay open until it closed its doors on the 15th of September 2013.

On the 9th of May at 11:28:34 UTC, user "baritus" said:

Hello Community,

We are fast approaching DigitalCoin's 1st birthday on May 18th. The important question is: how should we celebrate?

Let me know your thoughts!

In order to celebrate the one year anniversary, there were a few suggestions by familiar community members. User "teillagory" proposed that efforts be made to produce a mainstream Wikipedia page for Digitalcoin similar to those for Bitcoin, Litecoin and Dogecoin. Other people wanted a special giveaway to take place.

On the 10th of May, user "ShimalH" announced the release of Coinmart. At 18:28 UTC, he said the following:

> "We have not yet managed to fix the underlying problems with our Digitalcoin wallet. However Coinmart will still release today. Due to rushed nature of this release there are still some bugs with Coinmart, therefore we Coinmart is now in it's release candidate stage kind of like a soft-release. It will be done in the same way as CrypoAve."

Three days later, beta testing of a lightweight Java wallet had begun by user "HashEngineering".

On the 17th of May at 07:40:14 UTC, user "Swisscex" said:

> "Dear DigitalCoin community
>
> Please note that DGC is up for voting on SwissCEX: https://www.swisscex.com/voting
>
> Registered users have 3 votes every hour where as non registered users only obtain 1 vote."

Efforts were being made within the community to get Digitalcoin added to further exchanges such as MintPal and Poloniex. In addition, a growing number of cryptocurrency services were being contacted to adopt the coin.

On the 18th of May, it had been one year since Digitalcoin was announced on Bitcointalk. Two days later, the last block of the first year was timestamped to the blockchain. A total of 15,364,543 DGC had been generated up to this point:

Block #856,902 (Reward 15 DGC) May 20th 2014 at 09:56:17 AM UTC

APPENDIX

USER "BARITUS" INTERVIEWED BY BRENDON LINDSEY ABOUT DGC/SRC/ARG AND CRYPTOAVE PUBLISHED ON THE 27TH OF JANUARY 2014

DigitalCoin has long been one of my favorite crypto currencies, and it remains one of the ones I've picked for having the potential to be one of the biggest markets of 2014. But did you know that the creator of DigitalCoin is also behind two other prominent altcoins? The developer of all three — baritus — is no stranger to anyone in the crypto community. He's currently very busy setting up a new exchange that will allow users to trade his three coins as well as some others for USD, and vice versa. Despite his schedule, he was kind enough to take the time to talk with us and answer a few questions about DGC, SRC, ARG, and the future.

BRENDON LINDSEY: You've been no stranger to promoting DigitalCoin as being an extremely fair coin, both in terms of the launch and in terms of the block rewards not favoring early adopters. Why were those two choices important for you when releasing the coin?

baritus: It is important to establish a community on the principles of fairness, equality, and togetherness. When you have a good group of people behind a currency, it naturally attracts others and together you can build on a solid foundation. A currency needs to be focused on the longterm as well as the short term. We focus on the longterm through service development and providing a long lasting incentive to secure and use the network.

These days, it seems there are a few new alts each day, and almost all of them have a varying percentage pre-mined. Do you think that people are becoming too complacent accepting a pre-mine as the norm? Why do you think that is?

Many alts now a days are only concerned with making a quick profit and don't care about the effects of the pre-mine on the economy. Many people use these alts as games to pump and dump a large amount on unsuspecting and risky traders.

A lot of people see DigitalCoin and Worldcoin as "one or the other" investments, potentially because of both coins being the biggest named alts to be working on a crypto-to-USD platform. But do you think that's fair? Or do you think there's plenty of room for both DGC and WDC to prosper?

I think there is room for both to prosper. As long as service development continues and the community keeps growing, any currency can succeed. DGC is focused on remaining one of the most secure crypto currencies with a 100% secure record while at the same time providing a fast network. Many competitors have not maintained the same record.

You're widely regarded as one of the best developers in cryptocurrency. What's the key to being a successful dev? Do you have any words of advice for other developers stepping into the field?

The community is the most important aspect of any currency. They gives it value, secure it, and build an economy around it. A dev should keep working to improve the software, stay responsive to the environment, and work on services that add value.

Not only do you have DigitalCoin, but you also have SecureCoin and Argentum. What's your vision for how all three will work together? With three active coins, that's also a lot of development work. How do you ensure that all three remain successful and updated?

DGC and SRC are very different in that SRC can not be GPU mined. Eventually, there will be a miner client that allows users to choose what percentage of their CPU and GPU to dedicate to mining and the DGC/SRC will be mined automatically. ARG will be another option, with randomized rewards, for those that want to try their luck at mining. I update them whenever it is necessary and I'm pretty good at it by now ☺ .

Speaking of development work, let's talk about<u>CryptoAve</u>. What made you decide to work on setting up an exchange featuring your coins yourself, rather than rely one external exchanges like most devs?

CryptoAve will provide exchange capabilities to USD and other fiat currency. It will also serve as a reliable location where anyone can buy and sell DGC, SRC, ARG, PPC, LTC, and BTC at any time.

You've been in closed beta for CryptoAve since early December. How's the feedback from testers so far?

The feedback has been great. I've had a lot of software development experience and I know that testing is most of any serious project. It's especially important on an exchange and security has been my number one priority. We will continue testing in the Open Beta and add even more features from the tester's suggestions.

Were there any surprises encountered in creating CryptoAve? Or, overall, has it been a pretty smooth process?

It's been a predictable process but anyone who has managed a large project knows there are always difficulties. A lot of testing and perseverance later and it's looking great.

Once CryptoAve is launched, are there any other major development plans you have in mind related to DGC/SRC/ARG? Or do you plan to finally sit back and rest for a bit?

There are other projects already in the works. I'm working on gaming software that uses DGC for user balances.. More on that another time.. 😊 The Java implementation of the DGC block chain has been completed and a lightweight client is in testing by another developer, ShimalH. He is also working on a bitmit type crypto currency marketplace with DGC, BTC, and LTC integrated into the DGC wallet.

There are a lot of people currently getting into cryptos thanks to the popularity of Doge and other recent altcoins, and they consider anything released more than a month ago as "too old to get/mine". What do you want to say to those new adopters, to convince them to add their mining power to the DGC/SRC/ARG pools?

The more established currencies have proven their security, community, and drive. DGC/SRC/ARG have provided great returns to investors and remained secure throughout. There are a lot of gains to be made on all three but especially DGC, I do believe it is the most undervalued crypto currency.

We'd like to thank baritus for taking the time to speak with us. You can learn more about his three coins at their official sites (DGC, SRC, ARG). Stay tuned.

14th Oct article graphs by Hazard:

Network Hashrate (MHashes/second)

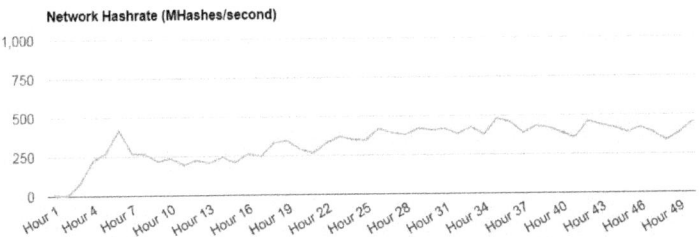

Total Supply

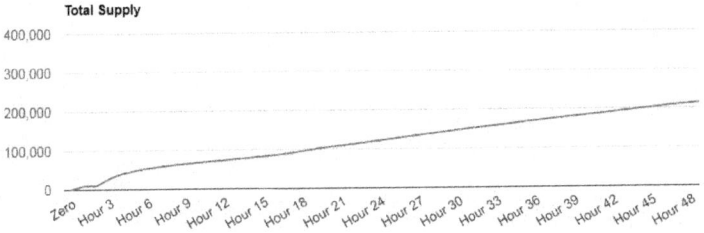

www.ingramcontent.com/pod-product-compliance
Lightning Source LLC
Chambersburg PA
CBHW070322190526
45169CB00005B/1707